BREAKFAST AT [illegible]Y'S

Truman Capote

AUTHORED by A. Kimball
UPDATED AND REVISED by Christina Shelby

COVER DESIGN by Table XI Partners LLC
COVER PHOTO by Olivia Verma and © 2005 GradeSaver, LLC

BOOK DESIGN by Table XI Partners LLC

Published by GradeSaver LLC, www.gradesaver.com

First published in the United States of America by GradeSaver LLC. 2006

ISBN 978-1-60259-053-3

Printed in the United States of America

For other products and additional information please visit
http://www.gradesaver.com

Table of Contents

Table of Contents

Biography of Truman Capote (1924–1984)

Truman Capote was born Truman Steckfus Persons in New Orleans on September 30, 1924 to 17–year–old Lillie Mae Faulk and Archulus ("Arch") Persons, a dissolute salesman. Capote's early life was marked by instability and poverty. When Faulk and Persons separated in 1928, he was left to be raised by relatives in Monroeville, Alabama, where he began what would become a lifelong friendship with Harper Lee, later the author of the renowned novel *To Kill A Mockingbird.* An unusual and observant child, Truman was determined to become a writer. He taught himself to read at age four and by age eight was "practicing" at writing in daily sessions. The details of the rural South, its oppressive poverty and wise, headstrong characters, impressed on the young Capote's imagination. He later drew on his memories of Alabama for some of his most famous writing.

In 1933, Lillie Mae, who then called herself Nina, remarried to a successful Cuban businessman, Joe Capote. Truman soon joined the couple in New York City, where he adopted his stepfather's surname and began an uneven career as a student in both private and public high schools in New York and Connecticut. While Capote was intelligent and highly focused on writing, he was uninterested in academics, and dropped out of his fourth year of high school when offered a 2–year contract position as a copy boy at the *New Yorker*. There, he attracted the attention of many of the city's literary and social elite, as much for his flamboyant wardrobe as for his mature, evocative prose. In 1942, Capote published his first short story, "Miriam", in the magazine *Mademoiselle*, which won him the 1946 prestigious O. Henry award for Best First–Published Story. He soon gained a contract with Random House, who advanced him $1500 for his first novel.

Other Voices, Other Rooms, published in 1948, was widely publicized, largely for Harold Halma's provocative back–cover author photo, which captured Capote lounging seductively on a chaise. The controversy surrounding the photo led to a storm of interest in the young novelist, and *Other Voices, Other Rooms* remained on the New York Times best–seller list for nine weeks. With his first novel, Capote became famous as a novelist and as a controversial figure who had captured the public's imagination. Capitalizing on Capote's sudden celebrity, Random House featured the Halma photo in their ads for the novel, which appeared in bookstore windows and continued to generate controversy.

Capote, now a celebrated member of New York's literary and social elite, followed the success of *Other Voices, Other Rooms* in 1949 with the acclaimed volume of short fiction, "A Tree of Night and Other Stories". In 1951, Random House published his novella, *The Grass Harp*, which he adapted as a play the following year. "Breakfast at Tiffany's: A Short Novel and Three Stories" was published alongside the serialization of "Breakfast at Tiffany's" in *Esquire* magazine, and proved so popular that the title story was quickly adapted for a major Hollywood film. With the publication of *In Cold Blood* in 1966, Capote secured his reputation as one of the most important American writers of the century. A novel–length exploration of the aftermath of the real–life murder of a family in remote Holcomb, Texas, *In Cold Blood* required extensive on–site research, and he took over five years to complete the manuscript. Serialized in the *New Yorker* in 1965 and published in hardcover by Random House the following year, *In Cold Blood* was an international best–seller and pioneered a new genre of literature: the non–fiction novel. Fragments from his final work, the unfinished novel *Answered Prayers*, were published as short stories in *Esquire* in 1975 and 1976, where they alienated the majority of Capote's celebrity friends, who recognized themselves as thinly–disguised characters in the work.

Capote's works are generally divided into three chronological periods. His early works are inconsistently styled with a focus on rural setting, family secrets and tragedy, and fall into the established genre of "Southern Gothic" fiction. *Other Voices, Other Rooms* and *The Grass Harp* belong to this early period. "Breakfast at Tiffany's" and its accompanying short stories, "House of Flowers", "A Diamond Guitar", and "A Christmas Memory" define Capote's middle period, which is characterized by a distinctively spare, direct prose style; minimal, linear plotlines, and a thematic obsession with eccentricity and the diversity of human love. This period also marks the development of what critics often call the "Capote narrator", the author's distinctive narrative persona who, while periodically participating in plotlines, remains conspicuously "objective", external to the story's narrative and emotional focus. The "Capote narrator" is also a distinguishing feature of *In Cold Blood* and the unfinished *An Answered Prayer*, the works of Capote's third period, which saw him moving towards his own, innovative hybrid of non–fiction and literary prose.

In his time in the public spotlight, Capote was renowned for his social stature and for his contributions to literature. His friends included actors, authors, critics, royalty, and aristocrats, whom he entertained in famous style. In 1966, in honor of Washington Post publisher Katharine Graham, Capote hosted the "Black &White Ball", a themed costume party widely regarded as the most important social event of the decade.

An open homosexual in a time when gays and lesbians were widely considered "deviant" or even criminal, Capote enjoyed an intimate, non–exclusive relationship with author Jack Dunphy from their first meeting in 1948 to Capote's death from liver failure in California on August 24, 1984. Today, Capote's life and works continue to capture public interest, with film versions of *Other Voices, Other Rooms*, *In Cold Blood*, and *The Grass Harp* released after his death. In 2005, the biographical film *Capote*, which dramatized the author's often difficult process of researching *In Cold Blood*, was nominated for numerous awards, and secured a Best Actor Academy Award for actor Phillip Seymour Hoffman's nuanced portrayal of the writer's struggle to maintain professional integrity in the face of his growing affection for the subjects of his work.

About Breakfast at Tiffany's

Breakfast at Tiffany's is Truman Capote's best–loved work of fiction and arguably one of the finest American novellas. Set in Manhattan's Upper East Side, during the final years of World War II, it documents the story of a young writer's fascination with, and affection for, his charming and troubled neighbor, the unorthodox Holly Golightly. The simple, linear narrative of *Breakfast at Tiffany's* provided Capote with the perfect vehicle to refine his characteristically minimal, naturalistic prose style, marking the novella as a transition phase between the author's more elaborate earlier writings and the documentary–style realism of his next major work, the non–fiction masterpiece *In Cold Blood*.

Capote composed *Breakfast at Tiffany's* in the spring of 1958, shortly after the publication of the critically well–received *Other Voices, Other Rooms*, his first full–length novel and a commercial success. Capote culled inspiration for his new work from gossip, personal experience, and the lives of his eccentric New York friends. The title *Breakfast at Tiffany's* is drawn from an anecdote popular among Capote's social circle about an ignorant out–of–towner who, upon being asked which glamorous New York restaurant he would like to visit, answered, "Well, let's have breakfast at Tiffany's". The author's idea for Holly Golightly, who, in the first drafts of the manuscript, was named "Connie Gustafson", likely came from several sources. In his personal correspondence, Capote acknowledged that he intended his charismatic and unscrupulous heroine as a composite portrait of a number of Manhattan socialites with whom he enjoyed intimate friendships, including Babe Paley, Gloria Vanderbilt, Carol Marcus, and Oona O'Neill. Holly's story arc, in which she escapes an impoverished childhood in the rural South to reinvent herself as a New York sophisticate, resembles Capote's mother's life. In particular, Holly's real name – Lulamae – seems to directly reference Nina Capote's own discarded birth name, Lillie Mae. However, as his biographers and critics have suggested, Holly was perhaps also a projection of the author himself, a vehicle through which Capote explored his own struggles with social convention, depression, and his need for permanence and stability.

Capote, already famous on the American literary and social scenes, found the market receptive to his new work. Shortly after completing the manuscript of *Breakfast at Tiffany's*, he sold it for $2000 to *Harper's Bazaar*, which intended to serialize it. However, executives at Hearst publications objected to the obscene language and explicit sexual references in the novella, and after demanding numerous revisions, decided against publication. While Hearst claimed that the colorful content of *Breakfast at Tiffany's* made it unsuitable for the pages of *Harper's Bazaar*, many of Capote's peers in the publishing world suggested that Hearst had feared the novella would offend or alienate Tiffany's, an important sponsor of the magazine. Alienated by *Harper's Bazaar*, Capote re–sold the manuscript to the rival magazine *Esquire* for $3000. *Esquire*'s serialization of the novella in 1958 appeared on newsstands at the same time as newspaper reviews of the complete novella, published by Random

House. The publicity surrounding Capote was overwhelming. *Esquire*'s sales skyrocketed, and the novella soon attracted the attention of film producers at 20th Century Fox.

Capote's novella was adapted for the screen by scriptwriter George Axelrod, who sanitized the work for a mainstream audience by altering plot and character details. Most notably, the screenplay reshaped Capote's complex narrative about sexual ambiguity into a conventional heterosexual love story. Released in 1961, the film version of *Breakfast at Tiffany's* was a star vehicle for Audrey Hepburn, who at the age of 31, was anxious about her flagging career. Wildly successful with both the public and film critics, *Breakfast at Tiffany's* revived Hepburn's star power and, thanks to the innovative costuming by legendary designers Edith Head and Givenchy, made Holly Golightly an instant fashion icon. As Capote's biographer's notes, the film inspired a legion of New York women to claim that they were the true inspiration for Holly Golightly. One woman, named Bonnie Golightly, even brought an unsuccessful libel lawsuit against Capote. However, despite Hepburn's vast popularity as Holly, Capote maintained that she was poorly cast in the role, which he felt should have gone to Marilyn Monroe.

Since the 1960s, both the novella and the film version of *Breakfast at Tiffany's* have remained popular with American audiences. While Capote's contemporaries gave the work mixed reviews, late 20th–century academic interest in the text has influenced its current public reputation as a piece remarkable for its technical innovation and progressive social politics. Influenced by the emerging critical field of gay, or "queer", literary studies, contemporary critics have been impressed by Capote's complex, sensitive treatment of human sexuality and gender roles. While earlier scholarship focused – often negatively – on the character of Holly as a personification of Capote's unorthodox views on sex and gender, modern critics have excavated the novella's subtle references to the alternative sexual identities and practices of the text's male characters, suggesting that Capote intended *Breakfast at Tiffany's* as an exploration of the powerful and loving relationships that often exist between straight women and gay men. As interest in the underground gay communities of the early 20th century continues to rise, it is likely that *Breakfast at Tiffany's*, and Capote himself, will continue to enjoy critical attention.

Character List

The reader is never informed of the name of the narrator and protagonist, whom Holly simple refers to as "Fred", because he looks like her brother. At the time of his friendship with Holly Golightly, he is a young writer struggling to make a name for himself in New York City. The reader learns little of his life apart from his adventures with Holly, which enhances his identity as a private "outsider" who, as Holly relates, "wants awfully to be on the inside staring out." An implied homosexual, the narrator later becomes a literary success and world–wide traveler.

The main character of the novella. At the time the narrator meets her, she is eighteen years old, thin, and has unconventionally short, boyish hair. A child bride who escaped her impoverished Texas roots at the age of fourteen, Holly makes a living as a companion to various wealthy and important men, who lavish her with money and expensive presents. As her name suggests, she is flighty and unstable. With the aid of the narrator, Holly escapes New York after she has been arrested for conspiracy with a Mafia–backed narcotics ring, and begins a new life in South America.

The owner of a bar located around the corner from the apartment building in which the narrator and Holly Golightly lived. He appears to be a homosexual, and prefers pursuing esoteric interests in dogs, radio soap operas, and Gilbert and Sullivan, over social interaction. Fascinated with Holly, he helps her flee the authorities following her arrest, despite his initial reluctance to get involved in the escape. He passes along a photo of an African carving that resembles Holly to the narrator twelve years after he had last seen her.

Another tenant in the brownstone apartment building in which the narrator and Holly live. A photographer for a popular picture magazine, it is implied that Yunioshi is attracted to Holly. To placate Yunioshi when he is upset at her for ringing his doorbell late at night when she has lost her key, Holly suggests she will let him take compromising photos of her. On a trip through Africa, when Yunioshi discovers an African man who has a carving that resembles Holly, he tries to buy it for a large amount of money and goods. Yunioshi also photographs the model Mag Wildwood for a major magazine shoot.

The man that Yunioshi encounters in Tococul, Africa, who has completed a carving that resembles Holly. The African refuses to sell the carving to Yunioshi, claiming that it is a representation of a young white woman who unexpectedly visited his village earlier that year. He implies that he had an affair with this woman, who later departed just as suddenly as she had arrived.

Often referred to by the narrator as "Madame Spanella". Another tenant in the brownstone occupied by the narrator and Holly, a "coloratura", or soprano, who enjoys regular roller–skating. Spanella often calls Holly a whore, and brings an eviction petition against her. Later, Spanella directs the authorities to Holly when they are seeking to arrest her. "Sapphia" is a variation on the word Sapphic, a common euphemism for lesbian. Despite what her name implies, Spanella appears to be a misogynist, accepting the same disruptive behavior in Quaintance Smith that she despised in Holly.

The man who accompanies Holly to her apartment door the night the narrator first sees her. He is upset that Holly won't let him come into her apartment and that she calls him "Harry". Holly explains to Sid that he should have given her more than twenty cents when she asked for change for the powder–room.

Holly's pet, a striped orange tom cat she picked up at the river whom she refuses to name. On the day of her escape from New York, Holly drops him off on the corner of a Spanish Harlem street, which she later regrets. The narrator promises to search for "cat" after she has left, and later finds him behind the window of a cozy Spanish Harlem home.

Holly's beloved brother, who does not appear in the narrative action. Holly describes him as "sweet", "vague", "slow", and over six feet tall, a height she attributes to his affection for peanut butter. Holly calls the narrator "Fred", as he reminds her of her brother. A soldier in the U.S. military, Fred is killed in overseas action halfway through the novella, a tragedy that causes Holly great grief. After he dies, Holly never mentions her brother again, and stops calling the narrator "Fred".

A major figure in the New York mafia incarcerated in Sing Sing prison on racketeering charges, and with whom Holly gets involved in a major drug scandal. Pretending that she is Sally's niece, Holly pays him regular visits, for which she earns $100 per week. At her visits, Sally gives Holly "the weather report" – statements encoded as information about the weather – which she then repeats to his lawyer O'Shaughnessy. Sally warns Holly before she is arrested, and Holly defends him in her public statements to the press on the day of her arrest.

A defrocked priest and gangster also known as "Father" and "The Padre". He is Sally Tomato's main accomplice in the scandal involving Holly Golightly. Telling Holly he is Sally's lawyer, O'Shaughnessy arranges for Holly's visits to Sing Sing, and pays her weekly salary after Holly has given him "the weather report". An obese man who seems addicted to hamburgers, Holly meets him frequently at "Hamburg Heaven". He is arrested on the same day that Holly is.

Holly's former talent agent. The narrator meets him at one of Holly's parties, where he shares the story of his unsuccessful attempts to transform Holly, whom he calls a "real phony", from a teenage runaway to a Hollywood starlet. He later reads the narrator's writing, and is unimpressed by its emphasis on description and socially marginal characters, which he feels will not "sell" with a wide audience. When Holly is arrested, Berman hires her a top lawyer on the condition that his name not be connected with the scandal.

A much–publicized millionaire who is the companion of Holly, and, later, the husband of model Mag Wildwood. Rusty became tabloid fodder at a young age when his parents died, leaving him their fortune. His godfather was arrested on charges of sodomy. As an adult, Rusty continued the family tradition of scandal with his three tumultuous marriages, all ending in divorce. The narrator describes Rusty as infantile in appearance and behavior, which Holly suggests is a projection of Rusty's repressed homosexual nature. He is hospitalized in the Florida Keys when he is assaulted by a group of young men, and marries Mag unexpectedly shortly thereafter.

Holly's on–again, off–again friend with whom she briefly shares her apartment. A model with a pronounced stutter and extravagant style of dress, the reader is introduced to Mag at Holly's party, which she attends uninvited. Holly implies to her guests that Mag has VD, after which Mag insults Holly and then passes out on the apartment floor. Mag describes herself as a "very conventional person" and is uncomfortable with Holly's frank discussions of sex. Hospitalized for sunburn in Key West, she suspects Holly of having an affair with her fiance, Jose, with whom Holly takes off to Havana. Holly deflects Mag's suspicion by telling her she is a lesbian, which provokes her to reject Holly. Mag later marries Rusty Trawler, and refuses to help Holly when she is arrested.

The fiancee of Mag Wildwood and, later, Holly Golightly. Jose is an important Brazilian politician who aspires to the presidency of his country. He is cultured, well–dressed, and attractive. Holly admits that Jose is not her ideal lover, but is happy to be having her first "non–rat romance". He appears to love Holly, but remains protective of his high social and political status. When Jose impregnates Holly, he makes arrangements to marry her in Brazil, but rejects her when he discovers she has been arrested. Highly concerned about his public image, he sends his cousin to retrieve his possessions from Holly's apartment and notifies Holly of his departure via a short, albeit heartfelt, letter.

Holly's husband, a horse doctor from Tulip, Texas. He searches for Holly in New York and gains the help of the narrator in securing their reunion. Doc reveals the true details of Holly's early life, claiming that he unofficially adopted Holly when she and her brother had run away from the foster home they had been placed in following their parents' deaths. A widower with four children, Doc married Holly when she was fourteen, and was despondent when she escaped shortly thereafter.

Upon their reunion, Holly sleeps with Doc again, but insists he return to Texas, alone, the next morning. Doc sends Holly the telegram that informs her of Fred's death.

The top lawyer O.J. Berman hires for Holly following her arrest.

The young man who rents Holly's apartment after she flees to South America. He entertains many male visitors and often has a black eye. "Quaintance" is a reference to George Quaintance, a provocative artist well–known within gay circles at the time of Capote's writing. Despite the indications of Smith's unorthodox lifestyle, Sapphia Spanella dotes on him, often nursing him when he has a black eye.

Major Themes

The psychological struggle between the need for stability and the desire for freedom is perhaps the central concern of *Breakfast at Tiffany's*. The conflict structures the relationship between the narrator and Holly, who are opposing forces. While the narrator is happy to have his first home, Holly is consumed by her need to constantly escape from places, people and things. Even Holly's identity is in a constant state of flux. Holly assumes the name "Holiday Golightly", which encapsulates her strategy of avoiding stability by making a holiday out of life, and abandoning relationships and responsibilities when they threaten to jeopardize her freedom. For Holly, the distinction between stability and freedom is articulated by two of the novella's major symbols: animals (including Holly's cat) and Tiffany's (in which Holly feels properly "at home"). Holly despises the caging of animals, and refuses to name her cat. As a "wild thing", she feels he doesn't "belong" to her. Her fantasy that one day she will have, "breakfast at Tiffany's," an absurdity since Tiffany's does not serve food, indicates her choice to avoid stability by casting it in the unattainable ideals of fantasy.

By casting the two main characters on opposite sides of the stability/freedom divide, Capote suggests that each has something to learn from the other. The mutual influence of the two friends is demonstrated by their Christmas gift exchange, in which Holly gives the narrator a bird cage and the narrator gives her a medal of St. Christopher. Each gift illustrates a median between stability and freedom: Holly's gift is a cage, but it will never imprison a bird, and the narrator's gift is a medal of the patron saint of travel, but it comes from Tiffany's, Holly's personal symbol of home. By the conclusion of *Breakfast at Tiffany's*, it is clear that this influence has, at least in part, been realized: Holly confesses her sense of "belonging" with her cat, and the narrator reveals that, since the conclusion of their friendship, he has enjoyed lengthy trips around the world.

While Holly and the narrator represent different psychological impulses toward stability and freedom, *Breakfast at Tiffany's* suggests that both characters' pathologies stem from the sense of social exclusion common to people whose lifestyles do not conform to American convention. Indeed, both characters are consumed with a sense that they do not belong or are not "at home" in the larger world. The narrator feels a constant outsider, his nose pressed against a glass, and Holly is convinced that she is a "wild thing", unsuited to a proper place in society. Thus, Holly and the narrator are similar insofar as for both of them, "home" has become a charged object of fantasy and longing.

Throughout *Breakfast at Tiffany's*, the act of naming is invested with special significance. The novella is populated with characters whose names or nicknames suggest their defining personality traits. For example, the "wild" socialite is Mag Wildwood, and the homosexual is Quaintance Smith, whose name references the gay artist George Quaintance. The abundance of meaningful names in *Breakfast at Tiffany's* draws a parallel between naming and personal identity that provides the reader with particular insight into the novella's main two characters. Notably, the narrator's name is never revealed to the reader, an omission that heightens the reader's sense of him as an "outsider" of both society and the narrative itself. Holly, also a mysterious character, changes her name to prevent others from knowing about her impoverished roots. Moreover, she refuses to name her pet cat, as she feels he doesn't properly "belong" to her. This statement indicates how, within the world of the novella, proper names symbolize both personal and public identity. Like the cat, the narrator's unnamed status in the novel suggests that he doesn't "belong" to any person or thing. However, unlike the cat, the narrator willingly withholds his name to protect his personal identity. Holly's use of a pseudonym and her reluctance to confer a name on her cat are thus symptoms of her general rejection of stability. She refuses to take or give a fixed identity until she feels at home in the world.

Many of the important events in *Breakfast at Tiffany's* occur on or around Christmas Day. The discovery of the African carving that resembles Holly and provokes the narrator to relate his story occurs on Christmas Day, 1956. On Christmas Eve, 1943, Holly and the narrator exchange gifts that confirm the strength of their friendship and symbolically articulate each character's desire for both stability and freedom – he gives her a St. Christopher's medal, and she gives him a birdcage. Finally, Sally Tomato dies in Sing Sing on Christmas Day, 1944, thus releasing Holly from her last pressing ties to New York City.

The motif of Christmas appears to be most linked to Holly, as her two pseudonyms – Holiday and Holly – are references to the "holy day" and the traditional plant of Christmas, respectively. Within the Christian tradition, Christmas is a symbol of rebirth, as the birth of the Messiah enabled His followers to be "born again" through His teachings and the ritual of baptism. Moreover, Christmas heralds the beginning of the Western New Year, a time which many feel holds the possibility of new beginnings. Holly's narrative presents her as "re–born" into different personae and attitudes at several key points that correspond to Christmas. The gift exchange (1943) confirms her presence in the narrator's life, Sally's death (1944) severs her connection to New York and thus the narrator, and the discovery of the carving (1956) marks Holly's final transformation into an art object that inspires the narrator's own art: the written narrative that is *Breakfast at Tiffany's.*

At the heart of *Breakfast at Tiffany's* is an exploration of the diverse kinds of love that define, enrich, and at times destroy adult relationships. In contrast to dominant social and literary representations of love, Capote's novella explores the validity and power of asexual relationships, often depicting such arrangements as more fulfilling than their romantic counterparts. What makes this distinction particularly interesting is that Capote suggests non–romantic relationships are not superior because they lack sex, but because they are not based on need or desire.

Breakfast at Tiffany's juxtaposes love and desire, drawing a sharp contrast between Holly's relationships governed by desire, and her relationships free from it. Her arrangements with Rusty Trawler, Jose, Mag, and Berman appear quite different, but all are based on need. Jose desires Holly sexually, Rusty needs Holly to fulfill his quasi–sexual infantile complex, Mag desires to share Holly's social contacts and apartment, and Berman seeks to profit from Holly's potential as an actress. Conversely, Holly desires what these people can offer her in return, be it money, professional contacts, or merely help around her apartment. While such relationships appear solid, all crumble, more or less, when Holly is incarcerated and no longer able to fulfill her companions' desires.

In contrast to Rusty, Jose, Mag, and Berman, the narrator and Joe Bell, both implied homosexuals, do not desire Holly sexually. Moreover, both are poor and unconnected to the New York elite. Consequently, Holly has nothing to gain from her association with them. Their friendships are based on sincere mutual affection, which Capote suggests is stronger than sexual or social desire. Accordingly, Joe and the narrator are Holly's only two friends to offer her unqualified support during her arrest, and even help her escape, endangering their own reputations and safety. Demonstrating the sincerity of the bond between a straight woman and two gay men, *Breakfast at Tiffany's* implicitly questions the narrow definition of love as heterosexual romance that is as dominant now as it was in 1950s America.

Through the character of Holly Golightly, *Breakfast at Tiffany's* explores one of the major themes of Western literature: the opposition of nature and culture. Holly identifies with nature – wild, untamed, and unknowable – over the structured, convention–bound world of human culture. Animals, both wild and domestic, symbolize Holly's rejection of social convention. As the child bride of Doc Golightly, her freedom from marriage is paralleled by her releasing her tamed pet crow. As a New York socialite, her self–sufficiency is embodied in her unnamed cat, a stray who Holly calls "an independent". The cage, a symbol of the human imprisonment of nature, remains an object of anxiety for Holly throughout the novel, and she refuses to even look at animals in the zoo.

While Holly considers herself a "wild thing", inherently unsuited to the rules that govern human culture, it appears that this is, at least in part, a facade. Holly is more than willing to be domesticated when she is offered the right price, and settles down more or less happily with the wealthy Jose. Her reliance on fine things and entertainment, and her worship of Tiffany's, a near–universal symbol of New York capitalist excess, indicates that Holly's appetites are not those of an animal, but a woman remarkably invested in the products of American culture. This ambivalence is suggested by another recurring animal motif: horses.

The horse is a long–established figure for human control over nature and animal instinct; for Holly, horses appear to represent her control over men. Her first boyfriend after running away from Doc is a horse jockey, she keeps volumes of books about horses on her bookshelf as "research" for her involvements with male suitors, and she fantasizes about running off to Mexico, where she plans to train horses with her brother Fred. She marks the end of her friendship with the narrator with a horseback ride, in which she demonstrates her skill as a rider. In each case, Holly has emotional or sexual control over the male character in the episode. When the narrator's bolts and runs away wildly, it prefigures Holly's loss of Jose when she is arrested later that day. While Holly associates herself with nature and the "wild things" she identifies with, the novella presents Holly in a more complex relationship with the natural world. In her relationships with men, she acts the part of both wild animal and trainer, achieving emotional and sexual control over her male admirers while evading responsibility and commitment.

Breakfast at Tiffany's is deeply concerned with the purpose of art and its shifting position in mid–century consumer culture. Holly is the novella's major symbol for art. Her persona is entirely self–constructed. Even her signature appearance is, as the narrator discovers, the result of deliberate artifice. Her hair is dyed, she diets, and conceals her poor eyesight with stylish dark glasses. Aside from concealing her true identity, Holly's self–fashioning implies that she sees herself an artificial object, an art work of her own creation. It is this artificial persona that the wealthy men in Holly's life pay for, establishing Holly as not only an art object, but as one that is sold as a commodity in the sexual marketplace.

Holly's willingness to sell her body and her image extends to her attitude towards art in general. She is particularly baffled by the narrator's reluctance to write primarily for profit. In the narrator's aesthetic ideology, art is a profound expression of personal and social truths and is thus unsuited to the often crass tastes of mass culture. Altering his writing to suit the demands of the masses would compromise the narrator's artistic integrity, something he is unwilling to do. Holly and the narrator are both artists of sorts; their difference lies in their distinct attitudes towards art's position on the popular market. Indeed, the characters' major dispute centers on the question of whether or not art is a commodity.

As with other differences between Holly and the narrator, the characters' attitudes towards art appear, by the end of the novella, to be less distinct. The narrator begins selling his fiction successfully. Holly, now symbolized by the African carving of her head, comes to represent a less commodified definition of art: the carver refuses to sell the carving to Yunioshi, even when he is offered a large amount of much needed goods and money. The carving is a personal expression of the artist's affection for Holly. Despite a lifetime of selling herself to the highest bidder, Holly's final image is not for sale.

Breakfast at Tiffany's is less a story about Holly Golightly and more a novella about telling stories about Holly. Capote articulates this focus on both structural and thematic levels. Holly is introduced to the reader through four layered narratives: the African's story, which he tells to Yunioshi, Yunioshi's story, which he tells to Joe Bell, Joe's story, which he tells to the narrator, and the narrator's story, which he relates to the reader. The introduction foreshadows the emphasis on storytelling and information maintained throughout the novella.

Throughout *Breakfast at Tiffany's*, the narrator's information about Holly comes from three sources: his observations of Holly, the stories she tells him, and the stories that others tell him about her. Often, the stories about Holly are at odds with each other or with his own observations, as when Holly's own tale of her happy childhood conflicts with Berman's account of her as a teenage runaway. That no "official" narrative of Holly exists exemplifies how, within the world of the novella, story–telling is distinguished from true, or objective information. Berman, Doc, and Jose all have different investments in Holly, and their stories function to communicate their own attitudes towards Holly rather than identify truth. The lengthy quotes from newspaper reports on Holly's arrest, which contain numerous exaggerations and errors, cast a similarly skeptical light on the seemingly objective information in the press. Perhaps, the novella suggests, there is no such thing as pure objectivity, and even information is a form of story–telling subject to distortion and personal bias.

In contrast to such narratives, the narrator writes stories that are largely descriptive: "not the kinds of stories you can tell". Aware that stories are inherently subjective, revealing more about the teller than the object of the tale, the intensely private narrator refrains from the kind of storytelling that the other characters appear to indulge in regularly. However, the narrative of *Breakfast at Tiffany's* is presented as the narrator's written recollections of his friendship with Holly. In light of the critical treatment of narrative throughout the novella, the reader is implicitly encouraged to treat the narrator's own words with similar skepticism. Rather, the reader is compelled to read *Breakfast at Tiffany's* not as a story about Holly, but as a story about the narrator and his investment in their friendship.

Glossary of Terms

A popular restaurant in midtown Manhattan.

A unisex cologne first introduced in the 18th century.

Mid–century slang used when someone has said something undeserving of attention or admiration.

Pierre Cartier was a jeweler whose name was synonymous with wealth and elegance for most of the 20th century. "Cartier–formal" thus suggests an exaggerated, "Cartier–like" formality.

drug addict

planning on disappearing

premiere

abbreviation of "razzamatazz", meaning a showman's routine

"make peace"

"the absolute end"; ultimate or ideal

An Australian song written in 1895 by poet Banjo Paterson.

One who believes in the absolute abolishment of all forms of government. In the early decades of the 20th century, foreign anarchists were often accused of plotting terrorist activity against the United States.

An extensive mountain range in South America

A profound feeling of anxiety and apprehension

Knit socks containing a pattern of diamond shapes in various colors.

singing in a low key

a luxury department store in Midtown Manhattan

Berlitz Language School, a popular institution for adults who wish to learn foreign languages, with hundreds of franchises worldwide.

Mafia

The Blue Ridge mountains, comprising part of the famous Appalachian mountain range that stretches across the Eastern U.S. from the Carolinas to New York State.

A large wild cat related to the American housecat

French phrase meaning "good journey".

French phrase for "close your mouth".

A linguistic system named after its inventor, Louis Braille in 1829, which provided an encoded tactile version of written language, thus enabling the blind to read and write.

bold

A type of building characterized by the reddish–brown facing on the exterior. A common type of residence in New York that has come to be closely associated with the city.

lesbians; "masculine" lesbians

lightness

19th century American frontierswoman renowned for her military skills and expertise on horseback.

A bright, coarsely printed cloth

The act of surrendering

To drink liquor in excess

roamed

critically

An essential oil often used to treat sunburn

An American composer who was very popular in the 1930s and 1940s.

A soprano specializing in ornate vocal music.

In a self–satisfied manner.

sick with consumption, a form of tuberculosis

Conforming to standard; not unusual or extreme.

derogatory slur for African–American

French word for "crisis"

A Hollywood producer, famous for his blockbuster *Gone with the Wind.*

depraved or corrupt

Fit skillfully together.

A small group of islands located at the end of the Florida Keys.

lesbians

obscure

French phrase meaning "and why not?"

A person who achieves sexual gratification by engaging in sexual behavior in public. More figuratively, an exhibitionist is someone who enjoys publicizing the details of his or her private life.

A type of Portuguese folk music characterized by mournful tunes and lyrics about the lives of seafarers and the poor.

An African–American spiritual leader who founded the International Peace Mission movement. Father Divine was the subject of public scandal when he declared he was God.

A soft, felt hat with a lengthwise crease down the center of the crown. While popular with many men in the early decades of the 20th century, the fedora was most often associated with mafia gangsters and private detectives.

A major thoroughfare in the center of the boroughs of Manhattan and the Bronx in New York City. A common symbol for American capitalist wealth.

Sign language

Greta Garbo, a Swedish actress who became one of Hollywood's most popular and highly–paid stars in the first half of the 20th century.

W.S. Gilbert and Arthur Sullivan, a team who wrote and produced several highly popular operettas or "comic operas" in Victorian England.

A type of flower.

nanny

German word for "housewife".

psychiatrist

The inheritor of an estate of a deceased person. Holly calls her unborn child "the heir" since he will inherit Jose's sizable estate.

Ernest Hemingway, one of the 20th century's most celebrated American authors.

ugly

here and there

payment

A chest in which young women store clothing and household goods in anticipation of marriage. Once a common tradition in Europe and North America, hope chests have fallen out of fashion.

Unbelievable; difficult to believe or imagine.

subjective; without concrete detail

severe or cruel

A period of warm, summer–like weather in the autumn season.

lack of motion; boredom

sickly

A very small amount.

Incense sticks often used in Chinese religious ceremonies.

A German composer of musical theatre and concert works who was very popular with U.S. audiences from the 1920s to the 1950s.

French word for "shit".

French slang meaning "African" or "black"

nail polish

A carefree or spirited adventure.

The site of Joe Bell's bar, presumably near 70th street in New York City.

go–between or messenger

A company that produced popular records teaching Americans to speak foreign languages.

medicinal ointment

A European–Jewish actress who escaped to the U.S. during the holocaust.

An expensive clothing line from the early 1900s which introduced the strapless evening gown.

cocktail drinks named after the New York borough, consisting of vermouth, whiskey and an optional dash of bitters.

An American Broadway and film actress who was popular in the 1930s.

A popular Russian actress who achieved fame in Hollywood toward the end of her career.

A slang term meaning "homosexual" or "male prostitute".

A type of thin, dry cracker that is often served with cottage cheese.

One of the world's largest and most important art museums, located in Manhattan, New York.

French endearment meaning "a thousand tendernesses".

tall, slender towers attached to a mosque, often containing balconies for prayer

Misinterpreted.

A division of Randolph House Publishers, founded in 1917. It's slogan was "The Modern Library of the World's Best Books."

temple for Muslim relgious services

A fictional town created by Capote, perhaps as an allusion to a gay resort or pick–up spot ("nancy" being a slang term for a submissive homosexual).

Jawaharlal Nehru, an important leader of the Indian Independence Movement and the Indian National Congress. Nehru was the first Prime Minister of India after the country's independence from Britain in 1947.

The fifth and final emperor of the Julio–Claudian dynasty of Rome. Nero was notorious for his decadent lifestyle and dissolute, untrustworthy nature.

Phrase meaning "to slobber"; plays on the derogatory attitude toward African–Americans in mid–century America

A western musical by Rodgers &Hammerstein.

A popular musical written by Kurt Weill which ran on Broadway between 1943 and 1945.

A rhythmic bass accompaniment to brass band music.

A town in New York that contains Sing Sing prison

A radio soap opera that aired on CBS from 1937 to 1939.

French word for unconventional or bizarre.

The United States' largest fine–arts auction house. Parke–Bernet was purchased by Sotheby's in 1964.

antiquated term for record player

A brand of cigarettes produced in New Orleans until the 1960s. The Spanish word translates to "something of little value; a trifle."

An abbreviation of "pidgin–English". Pidgin is a hybridization of two languages that occurs when both languages share close geographic proximity.

A maneuver in which a target is attacked from two or more sides simultaneously.

religious

Expressive of suffering or woe.

The popular acronym for *Picture Magazine*, a left–wing daily newspaper in New York City that ran from 1940 to 1948, when it was replaced by the *New York Star*.

neat or skillful

A breed of "toy" dog with a soft, dense coat and an excitable personality.

restroom

a pot that uses steam under high pressure to cook food quickly

a kind of stitch used in knitting

A U.S. military decoration awarded to those who have been wounded or killed while serving in or with the U.S. military after April 5, 1917.

to populate with military troops

emotional and extravagant.

A central New York location owned by the wealthy Rockfeller family, in which an enormous Christmas tree is erected and decorated each year for the enjoyment of the city.

A racetrack in Arcadia, California

William Saroyan, an Armenian–American writer of plays and short stories that documented his life in an impoverished Armenian family.

German word for "sleep".

A barbituate drug used to treat epilepsy and insomnia. Because of its sedative properties, it was popular as a method of suicide.

lawyer

A lawyer or politician who is professionally unscrupulous.

Georges Simenon, a Belgian author famous for his prolific output of naturalistic, psychologically objective novels.

A maximum–security prison in Ossing, New York.

In a reckless and haphazard manner.

A neighbourhood in northeastern Manhattan that has been populated by Hispanic–Americans for most of the 20th century.

A brief and sudden windstorm, often accompanied by rain or snow.

The patron saint of protection against lightning and pestilence. St Christopher is also considered the protector of archers, automobile drivers, and bachelors.

Light–weight hats, worn often in tropical countries as protection from the sun.

solid, earthy or bodily

a type of grain often used in desserts

Abbreviation for tuberculosis, a highly infectious lung disease whose severity is variable. A major cause of illness and death before the 1940s.

An electro–mechanical typewriter used to transmit messages across two locations via an electrial channel. Also known as a TTY, a teletypwriter, and a teleprinter.

an apartment building, often low–rent

A reptile turtle native to the U.S. that can live both in the water and on land.

A 1944 film about WWII starring Gary Cooper and Cecil B. DeMille.

A jewelry company named after its founder, Charles Lewis Tiffany. Popular since its opening in 1837, Tiffany's is widely considered the finest jewelry store in the world and has locations in most major cities.

weight in tonnes

To wobble or rock unsteadily.

French phrase for "completely insane".

A glass cup typically used for serving alcohol.

A popular antacid tablet.

Mid–century slang for "one quarter".

An English supporter of fascism and Adolf Hitler's National Socialist Party during the 1930s. She attempted suicide when Britain declared war against Germany in 1939, and died shortly later of complications.

A passageway or room located between the outer door and the interior of a building.

full

A British playwright, novelist, and short story writer. The highest paid writer of the 1930s.

A mixing machine made by Waring, the leading manufacturer of small appliances for home and industry in the U.S.

A silver–grey sporting dog originally developed for hunting.

A Republican candidate who ran against Franklin D. Roosevelt in the 1940 U.S. presidential election.

American newspaper magnate who is credited with inventing "yellow journalism" in the late 19th century and was a leader of the democratic wing of the Democratic party from 1896 to 1935.

Walter Winchell, radio personality and the first gossip columnist. The narrator here is referring to Winchell's popular column, which he wrote for the *New York Daily Mirror* for over 30 years.

A chain of five–and–ten–cent discount stores popular across the U.S. in the 20th century.

A novel published in 1847 by Emily Bronte, widely considered one of the greatest masterpieces of literature. It was adapted for the screen in 1939 by director William Wyler.

A Germanic language spoken mostly by European Jews.

A neighbourhood in Upper East Side New York. During the 1930s it was the site of violent street battles between Nazi sympathizers and anti–Nazi demonstrators.

Short Summary

Breakfast at Tiffany's documents the year–long friendship of a New York writer, whose name is never mentioned, with his neighbor Holly Golightly. The story is presented as the writer's recollections approximately twelve years after the conclusion of the friendship. Reminded of Holly by a visit with another old friend, Joe Bell, who is in possession of a photograph of an African carving that resembles Holly, the narrator relates that he occupied the same upper East–side brownstone as Holly over ten years ago. Shortly after he moves in, he notices Holly late one summer night when she loses her key and rings another tenant, I.Y. Yunioshi, to let her into the building, causing a commotion. He describes her as just under nineteen years old, thin and chicly dressed with a boyish haircut. When Holly begins ringing the narrator to let her into the building late at night, he is intrigued. He enjoys observing Holly at trendy restaurants and night clubs around town, and often watches her feeding her nameless cat or playing country songs on her guitar from his fire escape window. He even takes note of her trash, which contains numerous love letters from overseas soldiers.

In September, Holly visits the narrator's apartment in the middle of the night after one of her lovers turns vicious in bed. The two converse and Holly reveals that she has been paying weekly visits to Sally Tomato, a notorious gangster who is incarcerated in Sing Sing prison. Tomato's lawyer, O'Shaughnessey, pays Holly $100 per visit to convey "the weather report" – encrypted messages – between the two men. The narrator reads Holly one of his short stories, which she finds uninteresting, and the two fall asleep on his bed. She leaves abruptly when he asks her why she is crying in the middle of her sleep.

Despite this hostile exchange, Holly and the narrator reconcile, and she invites him to a party at her apartment. There, the narrator meets O.J. Berman, a Hollywood agent who relates the story of his unsuccessful attempts to make Holly the teenage runaway into Holly the movie starlet. The narrator also meets Rusty Trawler, a millionaire famous for his checkered family past who appears to be conducting an affair with Holly, and Mag Wildwood, an eccentric model who drunkenly insults Holly and passes out on the living room floor. Holly is upset with the narrator for not seeing Mag home safely, but he continues to observe Holly from a distance. He takes particular notice when Mag moves into Holly's apartment and often sees the two women leaving the apartment in the evenings accompanied by Rusty Trawler and Jose Yberra–Jaegar, a Brazilian politician to whom Mag is engaged.

Holly and the narrator reconcile when he shares with her the exciting news that his first short story has been published. While she feels that he should be more commercially ambitious as a writer, she nevertheless takes him out to celebrate. The two spend a day at Central Park, where they exchange stories about their childhoods, the narrator noticing that Holly's story is a fabrication. They later shoplift Halloween masks from Woolworth's. Shortly thereafter, the narrator spots Holly entering the public library. Following her inside, he observes that she is consulting books about the politics and geography of Brazil. Despite the deceptions and secrets that seem to trouble Holly's relationships with others, the two become close. On Christmas Eve, the narrator and Holly exchange gifts: he presents her with a St. Christopher's medal from Tiffany's, her favorite New York landmark, and she gives him an antique bird cage she knew he had admired, making him promise that he will never use it to imprison a "living thing."

Holly's inner circle crumbles in February, when Mag suspects Holly of having an affair with Jose on a group trip to the Florida keys. Upon her return, she and the narrator argue and she suggests his writing "means nothing" and is un–sellable. Protective of his artistic integrity and offended by Holly's crass commercialism, the narrator doesn't speak to Holly until later that spring, when the arrival of Doc Golightly sparks his sympathy for his former friend. Doc Golightly asks the narrator for help with his search for Holly, and reveals that he is Holly's husband. He tells the narrator the story of their marriage in Tulip, Texas, which occurred when Holly was only fourteen after she and her brother, Fred, escaped the cruel foster family they were placed with following their parents' death. Doc further informs the narrator that Holly's real name is Lulamae Barnes, and that she ran away from Doc and his extended family despite his willingness to indulge her often expensive demands. The narrator seems to re–unite Doc and Holly successfully, but Doc returns to Texas the next morning.

When the narrator reads that Rusty Trawler has married Mag Wildwood, he rushes home to tell Holly. He finds Holly's apartment in an uproar, the sound of breaking glass emanating from behind the front door. Joined by Jose and a doctor, the narrator enters her apartment to see Holly sick with grief and rage. Jose reveals to the narrator that earlier that morning, Holly received a telegram informing her of her brother Fred's death in the war. Over the next few months, the narrator watches Holly transform into a domestic homebody as her romance with Jose dominates her life. She furnishes her apartment, learns to cook, and gains weight. Over one of her home–cooked meals, Holly confesses to the narrator that she is pregnant, and that she expects to marry Jose and live with him in Brazil. This wish becomes reality, and on September 30, the narrator is despondent to learn that Holly is leaving for Brazil the following week. She invites him to join her on a horseback ride through Central Park. The pair are enjoying their ride when the narrator's horse is deliberately provoked by a group of young boys. The horse gallops off wildly into New York traffic, and is finally halted by Holly and a mounted police officer. The narrator passes out in shock. Holly takes him back to his apartment and bathes him.

However, they are soon interrupted by the intrusion of their neighbor, Sapphia Spanella, who is accompanied by two police officers. The officers arrest Holly on charges of conspiracy with Sally Tomato and O'Shaughnessy. The arrest is publicized in all the major papers, and with the exception of O.J. Berman, who hires her a top lawyer, Holly's society friends are largely unwilling to help her. The narrator visits Holly in the hospital, where she is recovering from a miscarriage induced by her vigorous horseback riding on the day of the arrest. He brings her a letter from Jose, in which he notifies her that, because of his political reputation, he is unwilling to continue their relationship. An upset Holly confides to the narrator that she is nonetheless planning on skipping out on bail and escaping to Brazil. She asks the narrator to aid her in the escape.

That Saturday, the narrator collects a few of Holly's belongings, including her cat, and brings them to Joe's bar, where Holly is waiting. Joe calls a taxi, and the narrator accompanies Holly on the drive. She asks the driver to stop in Spanish Harlem, where she leaves her cat on the street. The narrator chastises Holly, who is soon overcome with grief and jumps out of the taxi to search for the cat, who is nowhere to be found. The narrator promises Holly he will return to the neighborhood to search for her cat, and Holly leaves. While the authorities soon trace Holly's flight to Rio, Sally Tomato's death in Sing Sing makes her indictment unnecessary. Aside from a single postcard from Buenos Aires, the narrator never hears from Holly again. However, keeping his promise, he finds Holly's cat, now safely at home in a Spanish Harlem apartment.

Summary and Analysis of Section 1

Summary

The narrator reminisces about his first apartment in New York, a single room in a brownstone in the East Seventies. Though it was dark and "crowded with attic furniture", he remembers the apartment fondly, as it was his own space, containing everything he needed to "become the kind of writer [he] wanted to be".

The narrator reveals that his memory was triggered by a telephone call the previous Tuesday from Joe Bell, the proprietor of a bar located around the corner from the old brownstone. While the two men haven't seen each other in years, and while Joe doesn't give a reason for his sudden call, the narrator assumes that Joe has information about Holly Golightly, a woman who lived in the apartment beneath his and with whom he frequented Joe's bar. Despite a downpour of rain, the narrator takes a taxi to the bar, where he finds Joe alone on the premises.

After mixing him a "White Angel" (half vodka, half gin), Joe asks the narrator if he remembers a Japanese man named I.Y. Yunioshi. The narrator recalls that he was a magazine photographer who occupied the studio apartment on the top floor of the old brownstone and who, according to the gossip columns, had spent the last two years in Africa. Satisfied with his answer, Joe passes the narrator an envelope containing three photographs, all of an African man in traditional dress displaying an elaborate wood carving of a young woman's head, complete with short hair, large uptilted eyes, and a wide, full mouth. The narrator recognizes the sculpture as an exact image of Holly Golightly.

Joe relates the story of the wood carving to the narrator as Yunioshi told it to him the previous night. Traveling through Tococul, an obscure village in East Anglia on Christmas day, Yunioshi was impressed by a local man squatting in a doorway, carving monkeys on a walking stick. When asked to see more of his work, the African produced the sculpture of the head. Yunioshi, struck by the resemblance to his former neighbor, offered to buy the carving, but found the artist strangely reluctant to part with his work. Bartering salt and his watch, Yunioshi convinced the African to tell him the story behind the carving.

In broken English and improvised sign–language, the African revealed that the carving is a representation of a young white woman who, along with two white men, had rode into Tococul unexpectedly in the Spring of that year. The men were sick with fever and were forced to stay in the village for several weeks in an isolated hut while they recovered, while the woman developed an affection for the carver and slept with him on his mat. Then, as suddenly as she had arrived, the woman disappeared, riding off on her horse through the African brush.

Joe and the narrator speculate as to the truth of the African's story, and wonder about Holly's current whereabouts. The narrator surmises that the story is false, and that Holly is likely still in New York, either dead, in an asylum, or "married and quieted down." Joe disagrees, reasoning that he's been walking all over the city for the past ten to twelve years, and, given his fixation on Holly, he would have noticed her if she were around.

Joe having inadvertently revealed his affection for Holly, the two men share an awkward moment. The narrator returns the photos to Joe and rises to leave, but Joe grabs his wrist. He confesses that while he loved Holly, his feelings were not sexual: "[It] wasn't that I wanted to touch her." While, in his advancing age, he finds he has sexual thoughts "more and more", he insists that his love for Holly was that for "a stranger, a stranger who's a friend."

The narrator exits the bar to find that it has stopped raining. He walks around the neighborhood to the brownstone he used to live in, which, he discovers, has been "sleeked up", renovated with a new door and elegant shutters. Looking at the mailboxes, the narrator realizes that only one of his former neighbors, Madame Sapphia Spanella, is still a tenant, and recalls that he first became aware of Holly Golightly because of her mailbox.

Analysis

While *Breakfast at Tiffany's* is primarily the story of Holly Golightly, the novella's opening section places Holly at a conspicuous distance from the narrative action. The reader is told Holly's story after the fact, through the recollection of an unnamed narrator approximately ten years after he last saw her. This structural technique is called a "frame narrative": a story that encloses, or "frames" the central story, which then appears as a "tale within a tale". While the story of the narrator's meeting with Joe Bell is an explicit frame for Holly's tale, we notice this tale is also communicated to the narrator himself through a series of intermediary narratives: the African carver tells his story to Yunioshi, who relates it to Joe Bell, who conveys it to the narrator, who finally passes it along to the reader.

By introducing Holly in such an indirect manner, Capote calls our attention to Holly's essentially mysterious and enigmatic nature. Throughout the novella, Holly is characterized as an unknowable person: she operates under an alias, lies, and refuses to divulge the details of her life to her friends. The use of a frame narrative exaggerates Holly's mystery, turning her into a literal rumor that can be neither verified nor dismissed. Moreover, the interest of the narrator, Joe Bell, Yunioshi and the African in Holly's fate indicates the continuing power of her charisma. The African refuses to part with his carving, Yunioshi is willing to pay a seemingly unlimited amount of money and goods for it, and the narrator travels across the city in the rain at the mere suggestion of news of Holly. While Holly has faded into rumor, she maintains a potent hold on the imaginations of the men whose lives, however briefly, intersected with her own.

The opening section of *Breakfast At Tiffany's* introduces another central concern of Capote's writing: the ambiguity of sexual identity and orientation. Capote's novella was published in 1958, a time when homosexuality was a taboo subject that few writers addressed directly. Rather, artists often "coded" characters as gay or lesbian by implying they had an eccentric, or "inverted" sexual identity. While neither Joe Bell nor Holly are explicitly characterized as homosexuals, both are described in androgynous terms. The narrator lists Joe's interests as "ice hockey, Weimaraner dogs, Our Gal Sunday {a soap serial)...and Gilbert and Sullivan". Moreover, Joe is found in his bar arranging a bowl of fresh flowers "with matronly care" in a niche adorned with photos of hockey stars. This juxtaposition of the stereotypically masculine (hockey) with the stereotypically feminine (flowers, soap operas, musical theatre) suggests that Joe, like his interests, is similarly gender conflicted. In his conversation with the narrator, Joe, a sixty–six year old bachelor, insists he didn't "want to touch Holly", a confession that distinguishes his affection for her from the patently sexual infatuation of the majority of the men in the novel. Similarly, Holly is described as having hair "sleek and short as a young man's", and a "flat little bottom", stereotypically masculine characteristics that, along with her willingness to explore Africa on horseback, indicates Holly's rejection of mid–century gender roles, which, as the narrator suggests, would require her to be "married and quieted down."

At the time of the publication of *Breakfast at Tiffany's*, America was fraught with racial tension. In the wake of WWII and the dawn of the Korean War, Asian–American relations were particularly negative, and the increasing pressure for civil rights placed African–Americans under intense public scrutiny. It is notable that the opening section of Capote's novella features two important non–white characters: the photographer, Yunioshi, and the African carver, whose name we aren't told. Joe Bell, presumably white, refers to the carver as a "negro", an acceptable term for people of African descent in the 1950s, and to Yunioshi as a "Jap", a derogatory slur for Japanese people. The narrator's description of the sculpture as a "primitive carving" indicates the superior attitude of white America towards non–white cultures: the object is described as a "carving" and its maker as a "carver" (not, respectively, as "sculpture" and "artist"), and the adjective "primitive" exemplifies the common pejorative association of Africans with "savages" or cave–men. Despite the racist terms in which Yunioshi and the African are described, both characters are important in conveying information about Holly to the narrator, a centrality that foreshadows the eclectic and often progressive political atmosphere of the novella. The fact that Holly is rumored to have "shared the woodcarver's mat" (a detail Joe Bell is reluctant to believe) is particularly indicative of her liberal sexual and racial politics, explored more fully in the remainder of the novella.

With the exception of Joe Bell, all of the characters in the first section of *Breakfast at Tiffany's* are artists: the narrator is a writer, Yunioshi is a photographer, and the African is a sculptor. Even Madame Sapphia Spanella, the name the narrator recognizes on the mailbox, is a coloratura, a soprano opera singer. Holly, absent in person, is present in the carving: she is both the inspiration for, and the subject of, a work of art. A recurring concern of the novella is the role of art as a way to preserve, interpret, and even transform our personal experiences. It is the sculpture of Holly, as documented by the photograph, that inspires the narrator to write Holly's story and, thus, to explore his relationship to her and to himself.

Summary and Analysis of Section 2

Summary

The narrator relates that he had been living in the brownstone for about a week when he noticed an unusual card on one of the mailboxes: "Miss Holiday Golightly; Traveling." On a subsequent night at a late hour, he wakes to hear Yunioshi arguing with a young woman who has rung his doorbell to enter the building, having lost her own key. She finally placates Yunioshi by promising that she'll let him "take those pictures we mentioned." The narrator peeks into the stairwell and finally sees Holly: a thin, well–groomed 18–year old woman with short, multicolored hair and clean, healthy appearance. Behind her, nuzzling her neck, is a short, plump older man whom Holly thanks for seeing her home and then shuts out of her apartment. He argues with her through the door, upset that she has called him "Harry" when his name is Sid Arbuck, and complains that he picked up the check for her and her five friends. Holly "advises" Sid that the next time a girl asks him for "powder–room change", he should give her more than twenty cents, and he finally leaves.

Holly stops ringing Yunioshi's bell and starts ringing the narrator's at late hours whenever she has lost her key, which is often. Apart from these exchanges, the narrator and Holly don't speak. However, the narrator sees her on the town, once at a restaurant table surrounded by older men, and a second time dancing outside a saloon with a group of army officers. On his way home from spotting Holly at the restaurant, the narrator admires an elaborate and expensive birdcage in the window of an antique store.

In the absence of direct contact, the narrator spends the summer inspecting Holly's trash, finding that she reads astrological charts, smokes "an esoteric cigarette called Picayunes", dyes her hair, and receives love letters "by the bale". Watching her through his apartment window, he discovers that she has an orange tabby cat and plays the guitar, including several obscure country songs that suggest she was not from a city, but "pineywoods or prairie".

One night in September, the narrator is relaxing with a bourbon and a novel when he has the unpleasant feeling of being watched. He finds Holly standing on his fire escape watching him through the window. She is wearing only a flannel robe. He lets her into his apartment, and she explains that she has "the most terrifying man downstairs", who, in his drunkenness, has bitten her shoulder. Sitting down on a chair, Holly tells the narrator that he looks like her brother Fred, a "sweet and vague and terribly slow" boy who is now in the army, and the narrator agrees to let her call him by that name. The narrator reveals that he's a writer, and she reveals that she "trained" herself to like older men. When the narrator admits that he has yet to publish his writing, Holly tells him that she has connections that could help him.

The narrator fixes Holly a drink, offers her an apple, and he reads her his latest short story. She appears bored throughout the reading, and, upon its conclusion, admits that "stories about dykes bore the bejesus out of me". The narrator is too discouraged to explain to Holly that the story was not about lesbians. Holly confesses that she is looking for a lesbian roommate, as they "love to do all the work", and that she is "a bit of a dyke" herself; "everyone is: a bit."

Upon discovering that it is 4:30, Holly becomes anxious. She tells the narrator that on Thursdays, she has to catch the 8:45 train to make her weekly visit to Sing Sing prison on time. Holly confesses that she is visiting Sally Tomato, a notorious gangster who used to frequent Joe Bell's bar before he was imprisoned. Sally was never Holly's lover, but he admired her from a distance and arranged for her visits to Sing Sing through his lawyer, Mr. O'Shaughnessy, who offered her $100 a week for the service. Holly is pleased with the arrangement, despite the fact that she has to pretend to be Sally's niece and convey coded messages ("weather reports") between the gangster and his lawyer.

The narrator expresses concern about the arrangement, but Holly tells him not to worry; she's taken care of herself "a long time." She joins the narrator in bed and tells him to go to sleep, but he stays awake, aware of her presence beside him. Holly starts crying. When the narrator asks her why, she bolts out of his window, saying "I *hate* snoops."

Analysis

The second section of *Breakfast At Tiffany's* exits the frame narrative of the introduction and moves into the central story of the narrator's relationship with Holly. Capote develops several of Holly's unique characteristics, namely, her ambiguous identity, her unconventional sexual politics, and her artifice. To a lesser extent, the narrator is also elaborated as a character. Fascinated by Holly, he gathers details about her through anonymous surveillance: he secretly watches Holly out on the town and on her fire escape, and he investigates her trash. While Holly's is the narrator's story to tell, he is outside it, an observer or voyeur looking in on Holly's life. The narrator is thus established as a passive person, a writer who learns by observing others, rather than experiencing life directly. Moreover, he remains nameless (except to Holly, who calls him by her brother's name, Fred). Nameless, without qualities except those of the observer, the narrator of *Breakfast at Tiffany's* is the epitome of the objective, "all–seeing eye" of third–person realist fiction. The narrator's struggle to maintain his writer's "objectivity" in the face of his increasing personal investment in others is crucial to the novella, and to Capote's work in general.

Who is Holly Golightly? This question, which recurs throughout the novella, structures the second section. The narrator is intrigued by the card on Holly's mailbox, which reads: "Holiday Golightly: Traveling." The unusual name suggests Holly's unconventional nature. A "holiday" is a time of rest from the regular work–day, thus suggesting Holly's rejection of the Protestant work ethic that was prized highly in early 20th century capitalist America; "Golightly" is a compound of "go" and "lightly", which encapsulates her tendency to change locations, lifestyles and identities without hesitation or guilt. The word "traveling", which replaces the occupation title on the standard mid–century calling card, underscores Holly's flightiness, her temporary presence in any single location or relationship. Moreover, it alludes to the country song the narrator observes Holly singing on her balcony, which contains the line: "Don't wanna sleep, Don't wanna die, Just wanna go a–travelin' through the pastures of the sky". In the song, travel is presented as an alternative to death; Holly's calling card suggests that she "travels" as a way of escaping the deathlike banality of conventional existence.

However, the narrator's observations of Holly reveal that many of her distinctive characteristics are the product of conscious self–fashioning. In her trash, the narrator finds hair dye, indicating that her unique multicolored hair is "self–induced." The remains of "melba toast and cottage cheese" suggest that her fashionably thin figure is the product of dieting. And viewing Holly on her balcony, the narrator observes that, in addition to popular show tunes, Holly plays obscure country songs on her guitar. He notes that these are the songs that "seemed to gratify her the most", suggesting an unexpected rural background for the seemingly urban socialite. These observations imply that Holly guards her identity because, in part, it is a construction, an artificial creation that masks her more pathetic true story.

The narrator's conversation with Holly confirms his observations that she earns her living through unconventional means. She lives off the money her male admirers give her, not exclusively for sexual activity, but for her charming company in the bars and restaurants of New York. This, along with her short hair, candid discussion of sex and admission that she is "a bit of a dyke", indicates Holly's progressive sexual politics and positions her outside the strict definition of femininity that mid–century American women were expected to fulfill.

Holly's conversation with the narrator introduces another of the novella's key themes: the commodification of art and experience. Holly asks the narrator if he is a "real writer", to which he answers: "it depends on what you mean by real." Her response, that a real writer is one whose writing makes him money, along with her mention of Benny Shacklett, a writer of radio programs, indicates the difference between Holly and the narrator's definitions of art. Holly, a fictional person of her own making, is a woman who sells her time, affections, and even her body for money. She views herself as a commodity, as something that can and should be bought and sold. She *is* art as a commodity, and she extends this reasoning to the narrator's writing. The narrator resents her implication that the value of art is limited only to its success on the commercial market.

Moreover, Holly's visit to the narrator's apartment demonstrates the quick bond between the two characters, and foreshadows the friendship to come. Her affectionate description of her brother Fred, followed by her decision to call the narrator by this name, indicates that the narrator, like Fred, is someone with whom she feels comfortable and safe. The narrator's association with Fred becomes key to his dynamic with Holly throughout the novella.

Summary and Analysis of Section 3 &4

Summary

The following Friday, the narrator finds an apology note from Holly Golightly on his doorstep, explaining that she won't bother him again. The following Thursday, Holly leaves an invitation to stop by her apartment for a drink that night in his mailbox. He is relieved, as he has been consumed by thoughts of her all week.

When the narrator arrives at Holly's apartment, which is oddly void of furniture and has a makeshift appearance, he is greeted by O.J. Berman, a Hollywood agent. While Holly is in the shower, Berman explains to the narrator that Holly is a "phony", and tells him the story of how he met her. At fifteen, she had been living with a horse jockey in Santa Anita. Berman spotted her potential as an actress; he got her work as an extra in films and gave her French lessons to smooth out her "hillbilly" accent. But when Berman secured her an audition for a large part in a film called *The Story of Dr. Wassell*, she fled to New York the day before the audition, telephoning Berman only to tell him that she didn't want the part. Before Holly joins them in the living room, Berman tells the narrator that Holly is planning to marry a man named Rusty Trawler.

Within the space of fifteen minutes, Holly's apartment fills up with strange men, many of them much older than Holly. The narrator observes that the guests do not seem to know each other, and that Holly has "distributed her invitations while zig–zagging through various bars." The narrator amuses himself by browsing Holly's bookshelf, which contains only volumes about horses and baseball. He notices Rusty Trawler, a short, plump man with a babyish appearance, to whom Holly pays particular attention. Inside a book titled *The Baseball Guide*, the narrator finds several newspaper clippings about Rusty, which identify him as an orphaned millionaire heir who gained notoriety at the turn of the century when his godfather and custodian was arrested on charges of sodomy. The clippings further describe Rusty's adulthood, which was consumed by three messy marriages and divorces. Included in the clippings are tabloid articles that document Rusty's relationship with Holly.

Holly approaches the narrator and he asks her about her unusual selection of books. She reveals that it's part of her "research": "If a man doesn't like baseball, then he must like horses, and if he doesn't like either of them, well, I'm in trouble...he don't like girls." She tells the narrator about why she decided against being an actress: actresses need to abandon their egos. She talks about her cat, whom she refuses to name because they don't "belong to each other", and describes how she enjoys visiting Tiffany's when she has the "mean reds", a state of depression the narrator likens to *angst*.

Rusty Trawler brings the narrator a drink, and Rusty and Holly bicker affectionately when he complains that he is hungry. When the narrator comments that Rusty seems to be clinging to childhood, Holly explains that he "feels safer in diapers than he would in a skirt...which is really the choice." She tells the narrator that she advised Rusty to realize his homosexuality, but that he tried to stab her with a butter knife at the mere suggestion.

Holly suggests that the narrator resume a conversation with O.J. Berman, who has contacts that could help him with his writing career. She is interrupted by Mag Wildwood's entrance. Mag is a tall, eccentrically dressed woman with a pronounced stutter. She explains to Holly that she came uninvited after working with Yunioshi, for whom she was modeling in a magazine shoot. Mag flirts with Berman, and while he escorts her to the restroom, Holly suggests to the guests that Mag has venereal disease.

When Mag returns, she is upset to find the guests suddenly cold and hostile. She insults Holly and tries to start a fight with an older male guest. The party, Holly included, disperses toward the front door of the apartment. Preparing to leave, Holly asks the narrator to see Mag home in a taxi. As Mag rises, she passes out. The narrator checks her pulse and breathing, props a pillow under her head, and leaves Mag sleeping on Holly's living room floor.

On Friday afternoon, the narrator runs into Holly on the stairs of the brownstone, where she chastises him for leaving Mag on her apartment floor. The narrator is confused by Holly's sudden sympathy for Mag. Over the weekend, his confusion is deepened when a well–dressed, attractive Latin man comes to his door, looking for Mag Wildwood. Later, he sees the same man bringing suitcases into the brownstone.

On Sunday, the narrator sees Holly and Mag sunbathing on the fire escape, drying their freshly washed hair. He overhears them discussing Mag's relationship with the Latin man, whose name is Jose Yberra–Jaegar. Mag tells Holly that she is lucky that Rusty is American, and their conversation turns to the topic of national pride. While Mag is happy to be American and supports her countries efforts in the war, Holly is indifferent, and tells Mag that she plans on leaving as soon as the war is over.

Holly discusses her brother Fred, a soldier, and calls him stupid. Mag believes she is talking about the narrator, whom Holly also calls Fred, and admits that he looks stupid. Holly corrects Mag's mistake, but concedes that the narrator does look stupid: "anybody with their nose pressed against a glass is liable to look stupid."

Mag expresses concern over moving to Brazil once she and Jose marry. She reveals that while he aspires to be President of Brazil, she wishes for him to give up politics so that they can stay in America. Mag asks Holly if she and Jose appear to be madly in love to which Holly responds that it depends on his behavior in bed. Mag is embarrassed, but then confesses that Jose laughs during sex. Holly approves of this light–hearted habit: "most of them, they're all pant and puff."

Holly pressures Mag for more details about Jose's sexual habits, but Mag claims she doesn't remember: "they go out of my head like a dream". She claims that's the "normal attitude." Holly scoffs: "It may be normal, darling; but I'd rather be natural." She advises Mag to leave the lights on during sex, to which Mag responds that she is a "very *conventional* person". Mag calls Holly "a cold plate of macaroni", and Holly responds that while Mag has a warm heart, she is insubstantial. The two women bicker, both admitting that Holly would be better off in Brazil than Mag.

Analysis

The narrator's conversation with O.J. Berman expands the focus on Holly's artifice established in the previous section. Berman calls her a "phony", but "a *real* phony...[she] believes all this crap she believes." Holly's contrived, or "fake" identity and lifestyle is *real* because it permeates her life: for Holly, nothing is more natural than assuming different roles and personas. Berman's account of Holly's earlier lives as a girlfriend to a horse jockey and an aspiring Hollywood actress enhance the reader's understanding of Holly's chameleon nature. In particular, Berman's description of Holly's original accent as "hillbilly or an Okie" confirms the narrator's suspicion of her rural background while leaving the exact nature of her origin mysterious. The reader learns that even Holly's distinctive speech, peppered with French phrases and American slang, is contrived, the result of French lessons designed to "smooth out" her country accent.

At Holly's party, the fluidity of human sexuality is again put under scrutiny. In the opening sections of the novella, the narrator's sexual orientation is unclear; at Holly's party, it is suggested he is a homosexual. Browsing Holly's bookshelf and finding only volumes about horses and baseball, he admits that he was only "pretending an interest" in both subjects in order to gain a vantage point from which to observe Holly's friends. When he asks Holly why she only collects books on these topics, she responds: "If a man doesn't like baseball, then he must like horses, and if he doesn't like either of them, well, I'm in trouble anyway: he don't like girls." The narrator does not correct her, implying that he agrees with Holly's observation.

While critics of the novella have been eager to cast the narrator as gay, we must remember that sexuality in *Breakfast At Tiffany's* is never presented in reductive, straight/gay terms. Holly's discussion of Rusty Trawler in this section exemplifies the novella's exploration of sexual identity as being a fluid process that evades labels. When the narrator comments on Rusty's infantile relationship to Holly, she responds that Rusty simply "feels safer in diapers than he would in a skirt...[he] tried to stab me with a butter knife because I told him to...settle down and play house with a nice fatherly truck driver." Holly thus suggests not only that her Rusty's attraction to her is that of a child to a parent, but that his infantile proclivities are a defense against recognizing his homosexual nature. The impossibility of defining Rusty as either "straight" or "gay" indicates the novella's treatment of human sexuality as a complex and often indefinable phenomenon.

The third section also introduces three of the novella's main recurring motifs: Tiffany's, the "mean reds", and Holly's nameless cat. All three symbolize different facets of Holly's sense of homelessness and her conviction that she does not belong in the world. Holly describes Tiffany's as her antidote to a state of depression she calls the "mean reds" – not "the blues", but a profound fear of the unknown. Tiffany's, in contrast, is a place where "nothing very bad could happen to you": Holly feels at home in the store. Her cat, a wild animal she picked up by the river, is a projection of Holly's sense of not belonging. She refuses to name the pet, stating that she and the cat, "don't belong to each other: he's an independent, and so am I." She tells the narrator that once she finds a place that made her feel like Tiffany's, she would, "buy some furniture and give the cat a name." A sense of belonging, as symbolized by Tiffany's, is required for Holly to escape the "mean reds" and acquire a stable identity and lifestyle.

The fourth section of *Breakfast at Tiffany's* is short, consisting mainly of the narrator's observations of Holly and Mag Wildwood conversing on the fire escape. It establishes the fickle relationship between the two women, who had fought bitterly only a few days earlier. Through the dialogue between Holly and Mag, a "very *conventional* person", the reader's sense of Holly's unorthodox nature is heightened. Mag's embarrassment at discussing sex, her confessed sexual passivity (she prefers to leave the lights off during sex), and blind patriotism stand in sharp contrast to Holly's candor, sexual assertiveness (she states boldly that "men are beautiful"), and indifference toward her home country, a dangerous sentiment during the heightened patriotism of war time America. Holly's statement that she would "rather be natural" than normal indicates another recurring concern of the novel: that definitions of what is "normal" are arbitrary, and serve to control and restrain the natural freedom of the human spirit. Moreover, Holly's interest in Jose's sexual habits, as well as her statement that she would be better off in Brazil than Mag, indicate Holly's preoccupation with Jose and foreshadow the affair that occupies the novella's later sections.

Holly and Mag's brief discussion of the narrator, whom Mag confuses with Holly's brother Fred, confirms the novella's earlier characterization of the narrator as a outsider who observes, rather than participates in, his own life. Holly's claims that he "wants awfully to be on the inside staring out" suggests that she believes that the narrator's sense of exclusion is not his own choice and is, in fact, a source of despair for him. The narrator's position as unseen voyeur of Holly and Mag's conversation, literally "pressed up against the glass" of his fire escape window, ironically confirms Holly's statement.

Summary and Analysis of Sections 5 &6

Summary

On Monday, the narrator sees that the card on Holly's mailbox has been altered to include Mag Wildwood's name. He is interested in this development, but is then distracted by a letter in his own mailbox from a small university review. It informs him that the editors have agreed to publish his story in an upcoming issue. While the publication would not pay, the narrator is so excited that he forgets Holly's previous admonishment and knocks on her apartment door, eager to share the good news.

Holly comes to the door, clearly having been woken up. The narrator hands her the letter, and she takes a long time to read it. After offering her congratulations, Holly invites the narrator into her apartment and tells him she will take him out to lunch to celebrate. Waiting in Holly's bedroom, the narrator sees that it has the same "camping–out atmosphere" of the rest of the apartment, with no real furniture beyond the rather flashy bed.

Through the bathroom door, Holly tells the narrator about her decision to take Mag on as a roommate. While Mag isn't a lesbian, Holly explains, she is a "perfect fool" who had agreed to take on the lease and the burden of housework. Mag's modeling career means that she is out of the apartment most of the time. Moreover, Mag is engaged, which means that she and Holly will not be in direct competition for men. Holly explains that while Jose is a nice guy, there is a difference in height: "a foot, her favor".

Immaculately dressed and groomed, Holly treats the narrator to Manhattans at Joe Bell's bar. Hearing the good news of the narrator's story, Joe Bell offers them both champagne cocktails on the house. Holly and the narrator spend the rest of the day watching a parade on Fifth Avenue, eating lunch in the cafeteria park, and relaxing on the park's wooden boathouse porch. Holly asks about the narrator's childhood, and then relates the details of her own. The narrator notices that her own story, while pleasant, is "elusive, nameless, placeless, an impressionistic recital." He suspects that she isn't telling the truth, since he has heard that Holly had run away from home.

The narrator asks Holly if she had really run away from home at the young age of fourteen, and she admits that it is true; her previous story was a lie, made up because she didn't want to compete with the narrator's own tragic tale. Holly remembers that she wants to send her brother some peanut butter, and the two spend the afternoon haggling with grocers for jars of the wartime scarcity.

By the time Holly and the narrator have found six jars of peanut butter, it is dark, and the narrator takes Holly to the antique shop to point out the palatial bird cage he has been admiring. Holly admires it, but points out that "still, it's a cage." Spotting a Woolworth's, Holly drags him in, convincing him to steal something. The narrator feels watched, but, while the saleslady is occupied, he and Holly slip Halloween masks over their faces and exit the store without paying. He feels exhilarated, and the pair run a few blocks for dramatic effect. The narrator asks Holly if she had ever stolen before, and she admits that she used to, and still steals from time to time for practice. Happy, the two wear their stolen masks all the way home.

Analysis

Section 5, which covers the narrator's conversation with Holly as they are preparing to celebrate the first publication of his writing, mainly serves to enhance the reader's understanding of Holly's resourceful and opportunistic nature. The narrator learns that, despite the seemingly friendly relationship between Holly and Mag, Holly has only taken Mag on as a roommate because she thinks her a "*perfect* fool" who would be willing to take on the lease and do Holly's share of laundry. As she does with the wealthy men in her life, Holly takes advantage of Mag, and expresses no remorse over her behavior. That the narrator considers Holly to be amoral is indicated by his assessment of her makeshift apartment, strewn with packed crates he compares to "the belongings of a criminal who feels the law not far behind."

The following section contains one of most memorable episodes in *Breakfast At Tiffany's*: Holly and the narrator's idle, adventurous day in New York City. The section deeply explores one of the novella's major themes: deception. Sharing an intimate conversation on Central Park's boathouse porch, the narrator and Holly exchange stories of their early childhoods. When Holly tells a vague, impressionistic story of a happy childhood filled with "swimming and summer, Christmas trees, pretty cousins and parties", the narrator realizes that she is lying. Holly admits the lie, but does not seem embarrassed or remorseful. Holly's constant fictionalizing of her own history and identity, as well as her willingness to lie to her friend, suggests her status as a "true phony": a person who lacks a true sense of self, and consequently, a sense of moral obligation to others. Also notable in this episode is the reader's lack of information about the narrator's childhood, which Holly relates was a "tragedy". The narrator tells his story to Holly, but it is not recorded in the narrative. The withholding of the narrator's story exemplifies the dynamic of the novella in which the narrator remains more remote from the reader than Holly, whose story he is telling.

Both the narrator and the reader's understanding of Holly as a "phony" is tempered, however, by her frequent mention of her brother Fred, with whom she imagines settling down with in Mexico. The details about Fred – he is tall, good with horses, and loves peanut butter – are among the few true details of Holly's life she discusses with others. Her attachment to and honesty about Fred suggests that Holly is not inherently deceptive; but rather her lies are ways to keep herself invulnerable in the face of the "mean reds": her shattering sense of not belonging to other people. Holly's efforts in this section to collect jars of peanut butter for Fred despite its scarcity casts a sympathetic light on Holly and implies that she might yet be redeemed.

The theme of deception in section 6 culminates with Holly and the narrator's theft of Halloween masks from the discount store Woolworth's. Holly admits to the narrator that she once stole out of necessity, but now steals only for the fun of the deception itself. Her nonchalant attitude towards theft again positions Holly outside the moral standards of conventional society. Holly's choice of masks – a classic symbol of deception and artifice – as objects of the theft they finalize her status as a "phony", a person who would rather perform a role than living an authentic life. As the narrator flees from Woolworth's in his stolen mask, he feels a sense of exhilaration as he steps into Holly's shoes, abandoning his careful personality to briefly experience life as she does.

Section 6 is also where the novella's motif of the birdcage is explored in depth. As the narrator and Holly wander through Central Park, they avoid the zoo, as Holly can't "bear to see anything in a cage." Later, when the narrator shows her the birdcage he admired in an antique store window, Holly points out that "still, it's a cage." Pathologically anxious about being restrained by relationships or even a stable lifestyle, convinced that she belongs to no one and nothing, Holly's fear of the cage represents her fear of being imprisoned by others. That Holly's dislike of cages is introduced in Section 6, which explores Holly's deceptive nature, is important. By aligning examples of deception with images of imprisonment, Capote suggests that Holly's "phoniness" is a defense against making herself vulnerable to others, and hence, to the "cage" of an authentic relationship.

Summary and Analysis of Section 7

Summary

The narrator finds a full–time job, and sees less of Holly. While they are sometimes able to share an early–morning coffee on his return from work, Holly is frequently out, sometimes with Rusty Trawler and often with Rusty, Mag and Jose. The narrator notes that among such company, the reserved and respectable Jose looks out of place.

One afternoon while waiting for a bus, the narrator notices Holly entering the public library. Confused by this seemingly uncharacteristic interest, the narrator follows her in and observes Holly secretly from a nearby reading table. As he watches her take notes, the narrator is reminded of a classmate he had while in school, Mildred Grossman. While Mildred was a humorless, practical introvert, and Holly a lighthearted, irrational extrovert, the narrator considers them "Siamese twins": while most personalities are malleable and ever–shifting, Mildred and Holly "had been given their character too soon", and, as a result, would never change. Like caricatures, both Mildred and Holly were disproportionate embodiments of distinct "types": Mildred the realist, and Holly the romantic. After Holly leaves, the narrator walks over to her reading table and sees that she had been consulting travel and political books about Brazil.

On Christmas Eve, the narrator attends a party given by Holly and Mag. He helps them trim their enormous tree with baubles, tinsel, and stolen balloons. Holly tells the narrator that there is a present for him in the bedroom; on her bed, he finds the birdcage he had admired, decorated with a red ribbon. He is surprised by the amount of money she has spent on it – three hundred and fifty dollars – and she shrugs, explaining that it just took "a few extra trips to the powder–room." Holly makes him promise that he'll "never put a living thing" in the cage, and he agrees. The narrator hands Holly her present, a St. Christopher's medal from Tiffany's.

The narrator, speaking in the present, informs the reader that while Holly has almost certainly lost the medal, he still owns the birdcage, and has traveled with it across the U.S., North Africa, Europe, and the Caribbean. He recalls that the birdcage was at the center of a big argument he and Holly had in the February of the same year.

After the Christmas party, Holly, Rusty, Mag, and Jose take a winter trip to Key West. After she returns, newly tanned and blonde, Holly explains to the narrator that, soon after the group arrived, Rusty had gotten into an altercation with a group of sailors and was seriously injured, while Mag had to be hospitalized for first–degree sunburn. Jose and Holly had left Rusty and Mag in the hospital and went alone to Havana, where Holly became taken with their half–black, half–Chinese guide until it was revealed he was a star of a "blue movie" (pornography). When Jose and Holly returned to Key West, Mag and Rusty accused the pair of having slept together while in Havana, which caused particular tension between Holly and Mag.

Holly tells the narrator that she convinced Mag that she hadn't slept with Jose by confessing that she was "a dyke". Mag had believed her, and, to avoid sharing the same bed as a lesbian, was now sleeping on an army cot into the living room of Holly's apartment. The narrator gives Holly a backrub while she tells him that she passed along his short story, published in the university review, to O.J. Berman. She says that while Berman had been impressed with his writing, he thought the narrator was on the wrong track. "Negroes and children: who cares?"

The narrator dismisses Berman's criticism, but Holly admits that she thinks that the narrator's story "doesn't *mean* anything." She claims that *Wuthering Heights* was more meaningful. As the narrator and Holly argue, he realizes that she was talking about the movie version of Bronte's novel. Aware of his condescending attitude, Holly claims that if the narrator is to claim superiority, he should offer proof. When the narrator claims that he doesn't compare himself to Holly or Berman because they "want different things", Holly chides him for his lack of commercial ambition. "You'd better make money," she warns.

The narrator apologizes, but Holly continues to goad him. Finally, he points out the degrading way in which she earns her money, claiming that "Rusty Trawler is too hard a way of earning it." Holly tells the narrator to leave her apartment.

Analysis

The seventh section of "Breakfast At Tiffany's" extends the characterization of the narrator as an outside observer explored in the previous sections. The narrator spies on Holly, this time as she studies in the public library. Throughout the novella, the narrator vacillates between two distinct impulses towards Holly: friendship and voyeurism. In section 7, he explains that he finds a full–time job, seeing less of Holly; consequently, he finds himself again in the position of passive observer of her life.

Through the narrator's observations, the reader learns more about Holly's deceptive tendencies. After Holly leaves the library, the narrator discovers that she has been consulting travel and political guides about Brazil, the country Mag is supposedly moving to after marrying the Brazilian politician Jose. Holly's interest in these topics indicates not only her own interest in Jose, and thus her intended betrayal of Mag, but her ability to transform her basic attitude and identity as circumstance dictates. Holly was once credible as a jockey's girlfriend, a Hollywood wannabe, and now, a New York socialite. Her visit to the library indicates that she plans to transform yet again, this time into the cultured companion of a Brazilian head of state.

As the narrator observes Holly in the library, he is reminded of another girl he once knew: the practical, introverted Mildred Grossman. He conveys that the two women were opposites: Mildred a "top–heavy realist" and Holly a "lopsided romantic".

Through his comparison, the narrator reveals his account of human personality. While he believes that most people are malleable, their nature fluid and ever shifting, both Mildred and Holly were unchanging, their distinct personalities formed early and thus becoming unalterable. This is a provocative observation when we consider that Holly's identity is pathologically unstable and almost completely fraudulent. By suggesting that Holly's basic character was complete and unchanging, the narrator illuminates Berman's claim that Holly is a "real phony". Holly's fraudulence and instability is perhaps not a cover, but her true nature; her "phoniness" is a very real, essential part of her basic character.

Holly's account of her group trip to Key West further enhances our understanding of the fraudulent relationship between Holly and Mag. After Holly and Jose leave Mag and Rusty in the Key West hospital to travel alone to Cuba, Holly responds to Mag's accusations by lying, telling Mag that she was a lesbian. This lie is intended partly to defend Holly against Mag's wrath, and partly for the joy of the lie itself. That Holly responds to the narrator's shock at this deception with such flippancy – "I'm always top banana in the shock department...darling, rub some oil on my back" – indicates her lack of guilt over both the affair and her betrayal of Mag.

The argument between Holly and the narrator returns the novella to its earlier examination of the definition of art. Holly and Berman, both of whom recognize the narrator's talent, urge him to abandon his descriptive prose in favor of a style that will earn him money. The narrator, feeling intellectually and aesthetically superior to both Holly and Berman, feels that such a move would compromise the integrity of his art. At the crux of this argument are two competing definitions of art: art as a commodity (Holly and Berman), and art as a critique of society that is distinct from mass culture (the narrator). From Holly's description of the narrator's story ("Negros and children"; "description") the reader can assume that the narrator's writing, like Capote's, is what critics now categorize as "social realism": descriptive, objective prose that explores the social and psychological realities of marginalized subjects. While such writing was critically important, it was not often – with the exception of Capote – commercially successful. The narrator's disgust at Holly's plea for him to "make money" is thus an expression of his larger dilemma as an artist whose position in mass–consumer society is precarious. Holly, a commodity herself, represents the pressure of commercial society upon artists to abandon their ideological and aesthetic ideals in favor of economic profit.

Summary and Analysis of Sections 8 &9

Summary

After his argument with Holly, the narrator places the birdcage in front of her apartment door. However, the next day he sees it on the sidewalk and brings it back to his apartment. Nevertheless, he maintains his grudge against Holly, not speaking to her when they pass each other in the brownstone or at Joe Bell's. However, when Sapphia Spanella, another tenant, brings a petition against Holly to have her evicted, the narrator refuses to sign, and the petition fails.

Later that spring, the narrator notices a suspicious man looking at Holly's mailbox. He is in his late–fifties and shabbily dressed. The narrator sees the man throughout the day, and realizes that he is following him. When the man sits down beside him in a restaurant, the narrator asks him what he wants, and the man tells him he is looking for a friend. The man shows the narrator a photo of himself and several children standing on a weathered porch. He points out that one of the children is Holly, and that another is her brother Fred. The man tells the narrator that he is a horse doctor from Texas named Doc Golightly, and that Holly's real name is Lulamae Barnes. They were married when Holly was thirteen. Doc was informed of his wife's whereabouts by Fred, and intends to convince Holly to return to him and the children he is raising from his first marriage.

Doc explains that he first encountered Holly and Fred when they were attempting to steal milk and turkey eggs from his farm. They had run away from the family they had been placed with when their parents died of tuberculosis. Doc took pity on the children and raised them as his own. Impressed by Holly's intelligence and charm, he eventually proposed to her. While she was well fed and did little housework, preferring to "comb her hair and send away for all the magazines," Holly was restless and eventually ran away.

Doc asks the narrator to let Holly know that he is here, and the narrator agrees. The two men return to the brownstone, where Doc waits at the bottom of the stairs while the narrator knocks on Holly's door. Holly assumes that he has come to make up after their fight, and asks him to return the next day, but when he calls her "Lulamae", she realizes that he has heard about her true identity. Thinking that it is her brother who is visiting, she calls down the hall for Fred. When she sees Doc, they laugh and embrace happily while Madame Spanella looks on with disapproval.

The next morning, Holly and the narrator have a conversation at Joe Bell's bar. She explains that she doesn't need to divorce Doc since she was only fourteen when she married, and thus, the marriage wasn't legal. She confesses that while she never intended to return to Texas with Doc, she slept with him the night before, since he gave her confidence as a child, and "anyone who ever gave you confidence, you owe them a lot." She explains that she took him to the bus station that morning, and, as they were saying goodbye, she realized that was still Lulamae, "stealing turkey eggs and running through a brier patch."

"Never love a wild thing," Holly tells Joe. She explains that Doc was always nurturing wild animals, and that the more love he gave them, the stronger they became. Drunkenly, Holly states that "if you let yourself love a wild thing...[you'll] end up looking at the sky." Realizing that her husband must be back in Texas already, Holly invites the narrator to join her in a toast to Doc.

Analysis

The narrator's attachment to Holly is revealed in Section 8 through his ambivalent behavior. While he claims to desire Holly out of his life, he rescues the birdcage she gave him from the sidewalk curb, and refuses to sign a petition that would have her evicted. He is willing to act like he is angry, but unwilling to do anything that would sever his ties with Holly. Rather than true anger, the narrator appears to be performing anger as a way of working through his conflicted feelings toward her.

The appearance of Doc Golightly in this section re–establishes the ties between the narrator and Holly, not merely because the narrator acts as a liaison for Doc and Holly but because it reveals to the narrator the secret of Holly's early life, thereby making her vulnerable to the narrator. Not only does the narrator learn of the poverty and abuse of Holly's childhood, which explains her perpetual sense of homelessness, but he also learns her real name – Lulamae Barnes – which no one else seems to know. Holly's true story is exposed to the narrator, and thus she can't afford to maintain a grudge. Moreover, knowing Holly's true identity gives the narrator an upper hand over her and triggers his protective instinct toward his friend.

It is interesting that Holly's real name – Lulamae – is quite similar to Capote's own mother's name, Lillie Mae. Like Holly, Capote's mother changed her name to a more sophisticated sounding one – Nina – when she moved from the rural south to New York City. Lulamae, a compound of the names "Lula" and "Mae", alludes to springtime; it is interesting that Holly replaced it with a name that refers to a winter plant. The opposing meanings of the two names encapsulates the severity with which Holly rejects her roots, constructing a new identity that is the complete opposite of the one she was born with.

However, Holly's conversation with the narrator in Joe's bar the morning following Doc's visit indicates she has not been affected by the return of her secret past. She admits to having slept with her husband again, not out of love, but because she felt she still "owed" him for having rescued her and her brother. As she does with the men she entertains in New York, Holly sells her body to Doc as a kind of payment for his kindness, and does so with nonchalance. Doc was not angry with Holly and still hoped for her return again, which indicates her power over the men in her life, doubly illustrated by the narrator's renewed devotion.

Holly's drunken monologue in Joe's bar is one of the novella's famous passages. It gives the reader further insight into the initial attraction between Doc and the young Holly. She explains that Doc was "always hauling home wild things...a hawk with a hurt wing...a full–grown bobcat with a broken leg." He loved to nurture and nurse these animals, despite the fact they only abandoned him once they were back to health. "Never love a wild thing," Holly warns Joe, "[you'll] end up looking at the sky." Holly, a starving and homeless child when Doc adopted her, is thus aligned with the wild animals he also loved. Considering herself a "wild thing", she indicates that she believes that, like an animal, she is inherently untamable, and that it is her essential nature to run away from those who love her. In this way, Holly admits to her fear of commitment while suggesting that, like an animal, she is not responsible for her behavior. Directing her warning at Joe, Holly subtly indicates that he should prepare to be hurt when she inevitably leaves her life in New York.

Summary and Analysis of Sections 10 &11

Summary

Returning by subway from a job interview, the narrator sees a passenger reading a newspaper with the headline "Trawler Marries Fourth". He assumes that Trawler's bride is Holly, and is surprised. He explains that he hasn't seen Holly since the Sunday following Doc's visit, having been depressed after losing his job and learning that he may be drafted into the war effort.

Thinking about Holly and Rusty, the narrator is disappointed. He realizes that he is a little in love with Holly, in the way that he was once in love with his family cook and a neighborhood postman as a child. His love for her is no less potent for being unromantic or asexual. "That category of love generates jealousy, too," he explains.

At the next subway station, the narrator buys a newspaper and discovers to his relief that Rusty has not married Holly, but Mag Wildwood. When he returns to the brownstone, he finds Sapphia Spanella raving in the hallway, begging him to call the police. From behind Holly's door, the narrator hears the sound of crashing glass and furniture being overturned. He is soon joined by Jose, who brings a doctor. Jose opens the door with his own key. Inside, the three men find the apartment wrecked, all the contents smashed, and Holly lying on the bed in a stupor. The doctor injects Holly with a sedative while she rants incoherently about her brother, Fred.

While the doctor attends to Holly, the narrator and Jose discuss her outburst. Jose confesses that, given his high political office, he can't afford a public scandal. The narrator assumes that Holly's tantrum was provoked by Rusty's marriage to Mag, and Jose corrects him by passing him a telegram from Doc Golightly in Texas, which informs Holly that her brother Fred was killed in action.

The narrator relates that Holly never mentioned her brother again and stopped calling him Fred. Over the summer, Holly becomes a recluse, letting her hair darken and putting on weight. Jose moves into the apartment, though he is often in Washington. Nevertheless, the narrator explains, Holly seems happier, content learning to keep house, furnish her apartment, and speak Portuguese. She cooks elaborate, unsuccessful meals for Jose and the narrator, and begins talking about her future as Jose's wife. Holly confesses to the narrator that she is six weeks pregnant.

Elaborating on her devotion to Jose, Holly tells the narrator that though she has only had eleven lovers, she is happy to be leaving her promiscuous lifestyle behind. She tells him that she is tired of pretending to love men that she knew were "rats", and that excluding Doc, Jose was her "first non–rat romance." While Jose is not Holly's ideal man, she loves him, and caring for him gives her a sense of satisfaction.

Through the final weeks of summer, the narrator and Holly become closer, learning to communicate in silence. When Jose is out of town, he and Holly take walks to Chinatown and watch ships from the Brooklyn Bridge. Holly tells him that, one day in the future, she will return to New York on one of those ships, "me and my nine Brazilian brats." She confesses that she loves New York, even though the city doesn't belong to her and she doesn't belong to it. The narrator explains that he felt suddenly left out as Holly continued on her lifelong travels.

Analysis

Section 10 marks the first point in their friendship where the narrator realizes he is in love with Holly. Jealous of what he assumes is Holly's marriage to Rusty Trawler, the narrator begins to explore his feelings about her. He compares his love for her to the affection he felt for his family cook, his neighborhood mailman, and "a whole family named McKendrick." He suggests that this love was nonetheless powerful because it was non sexual, therein touching on another of the novella's main themes: the diversity and validity of loving relationships among adults. Moreover, in clarifying the asexual nature of his feelings for Holly, the narrator again implies that he is a homosexual.

Upon hearing of her brother's death, Holly's behavior is violent and self–destructive. She smashes glass and upturns all her furniture in a fit of despair, not caring who hears and without regard for the consequences. While Holly had described her bouts of the "mean reds", her behavior throughout the novella is remarkably upbeat and nonchalant, illustrating her minimal personal investment in her relationships. However, her rage at Fred's death indicates that her attachment to her brother was quite real and strong. The extremity of Holly's despair further suggests why she avoids permanent relationships, as her experience of pain is apparently intense and self–destructive. Avoiding real attachments is perhaps Holly's way to protect herself against the kind of pain she feels at her brother's death.

Fred appears to symbolize Holly's sense of freedom; a recurrent fantasy of hers was that the two of them would escape to Mexico, where they would raise horses. Accordingly, at Fred's death, Holly allows Jose to move in, thus "caging" her in her own apartment. She transforms herself into an "un–Holly–like" version of a stable, domestic housewife. She furnishes her apartment – something she claimed she wouldn't do until she felt she "belonged" – and stops dying her signature multi–colored hair. She becomes pregnant and attempts to learn cooking and Portuguese. She repeats to the narrator that she is happy and that she loves Jose, claims that appear too emphatic to be entirely sincere.

In an extended monologue, Holly justifies her reasons for settling down, claiming that she was tired of her promiscuous lifestyle, "rat" boyfriends, and her bouts of the "mean reds". Section 11 thus documents another of Holly's transformations. Yet, while Holly seems happy, the narrator is unconvinced that she has indeed settled down. He notes that while she is proud of her cooking, it is actually awful. The disjunction here between Holly's thoughts and reality indicates that, unlike her role as a socialite, "domestic wife" is a fictional part that Holly plays badly.

While section 11 ostensibly deals with Holly's transformation, it is implicitly concerned with the narrator's particular character flaw: his reluctance to be anything but a passive observer of his own life. While he recognizes that he loves Holly, he does not tell her this, and rather allows her to settle into a relationship with Jose that could take her to Brazil forever. The narrator's passivity is, in fact, exaggerated in this section by the fact that he has no dialogue apart from his telling Holly "do shut up." This remark is provoked by a sudden anger at his feeling "left out – a tugboat in dry dock while she, glittery voyager of secure destination, steamed down the harbor." The narrator recognizes his perpetual feeling of exclusion is, like a boat moored to a dock, holding him back. However, he does not take direct action to change this quality.

The final metaphor of the section, which compares the narrator's final days with Holly to autumn leaves blowing in the wind, indicates the banality of Holly's new personality. Like leaves, the narrator can't tell the days apart, as they are all alike. The reference to autumn leaves, which are on the verge of death, symbolizes the end of the narrator's friendship with Holly.

Summary and Analysis of Sections 12 &13

Summary

On the 30th of September, the narrator's birthday, he waits in the vestibule of the brownstone for the postman, whom he hopes will be bringing money from his family. He runs into Holly, who invites him to go horseback riding as a last outing before she leaves to marry Jose in Brazil. She explains that she can't leave New York without saying goodbye to her favorite horse, Mabel Minerva.

The two take a taxi to Central Park. On the way, Holly explains that she will miss him, as well as Sally Tomato, who had warned her that the authorities suspected she was not his real niece. She tells him that O'Shaughnessy gave her $500 as a wedding present. The narrator, upset that she is leaving so suddenly, tries to tell her that she is already married, but she threatens to hang him if reveals that information and jeopardizes her marriage to Jose.

At the stables, Holly selects a sedate mare for the narrator, who is an inexperienced rider, while she mounts Mabel Minerva. As they ride across Central Park, the narrator is overcome with love for Holly, and realizes that his desire for her happiness is greater than his own need to keep her with him. This moment of exhilaration is cut short when a group of African–American boys leap out of the shrubbery and begin throwing rocks and taunting the horses. The narrator's horse rises on her hind legs and begins a violent gallop across the park and out into Fifth Avenue traffic.

Eventually, the narrator's runaway horse is brought to a halt by a mounted police officer and Holly, who has been following on Mabel Minerva. As a crowd gathers, the officer takes notes and arranges for the horses to be returned to the stables. Holly tells the narrator that he could have been killed, but he insists that he is only ashamed. When she kisses his cheek, however, he becomes dizzy and passes out on the sidewalk.

Back in his apartment, the narrator recovers in a bath while Holly sits on the edge of the tub, waiting to rub him with liniment. Sapphia Spanella knocks on the door and then enters, followed by two plain–clothes detectives, one male and one female. She points to Holly and identifies her as "the wanted woman". The female detective places her hand on Holly's shoulder and tells her kindly to "come along", but Holly warns her not to touch her, calling her a "driveling old bull–dyke." The officer slaps Holly, and the bottle of liniment flies from her hand and breaks on the floor. As Holly is escorted out of the apartment, she asks the narrator to feed her cat.

By that evening, the news of Holly's arrest is on all the front pages of the daily newspapers. To the narrator's surprise, the news had nothing to do with runaway horses; rather, Holly was implicated in a drug smuggling operation as an accomplice to Sally Tomato. O'Shaughnessy was also arrested, and revealed to be not a lawyer but a defrocked priest with a history of arrests for mafia activity. According to the press, Holly had been accused of acting as a liaison between Sally and O'Shaughnessy, conveying coded messages between the two men that allowed them to maintain control over a world–wide narcotics syndicate.

The narrator notices how the coverage distorts Holly's story for sensational effect, calling her a "movie starlet" when she was only an extra in films and claiming that she was arrested in "her luxurious apartment" when she was arrested in his own bathroom. One paper runs a story under the subheading "Admits Own Drug Addiction": while denying her knowledge of the narcotics ring to reporters, she admitted to having used marijuana. The papers also inform that narrator that despite her arrest, Holly remains unconvinced of Sally's guilt. "He's a sensitive, a religious person," she tells the reporters. "A darling old man."

Analysis

Section 12 depicts the narrator achieving closure over his grief at Holly's sudden departure. Holly convinces the narrator to go horseback riding, marking the final appearance of horses as a recurrent motif in the novella. Holly associates horses with her brother Fred, stating that she imagined settling down with him in Mexico to raise horses. As Holly and the narrator ride alongside each other, they both experience an exhilarating high, and, seeing Holly's happiness, realizes that he loves her so much that he values her happiness above his own, even if that means the end of their friendship. By placing him on a horse, Capote subtly aligns him with Holly's brother Fred, a person with whom she felt safe and cared for. This association suggests the strength of the emotional bond between the narrator and Holly.

The section also sets the two characters up for contrast. Holly and the narrator's description of the horseback ride – "a glad–to–be–alive exhilaration" – echoes that of the mask theft at Woolworth's. The similar language links the two excursions and sets them up for comparison. As during the escape from Woolworth's, the narrator challenges his own boundaries and breaks habit by engaging in one of Holly's typically "carefree" activities. His pure happiness during both the theft and the horseback ride indicates that Holly's unconventional and spontaneous attitude is what is missing from the narrator's own life, and suggests that his attachment to Holly is partly a wish to become more like her.

However, while the Woolworth's theft ends smoothly, the horseback ride soon becomes dangerous, as the narrator's horse gallops into traffic and endangers his life. This near–tragic end to Holly and the narrator's last adventure serves two purposes. First, it confirms the bond between the two characters when Holly successfully halts the narrator's runaway horse, despite such vigorous riding endangering her pregnancy. Moreover, Holly's rescue of the narrator foreshadows the concluding events of the novella, in which the narrator helps Holly escape from the law.

Section 13 is a structural departure from the rest of the novella. *Breakfast at Tiffany's* is a linear narrative: events are told in the order in which they happen. In section 13, the order is reversed: the reader is told about the consequences of Holly's arrest before the arrest itself. Moreover, the majority of the section directly quotes newspaper coverage of the arrest. Up until this section, the events of Holly's life had been conveyed to the reader through the narrator. This switch of perspective violates the reader's expectations. Section 13's non–linear narrative and an external source of information is surprising, as it upturns the established method of the novella. Capote uses an unexpected structure that mirrors the shocking turn of events.

A central concern of *Breakfast at Tiffany's* is the impossibility of objectivity. Lies, gossip, and stories, all claiming to be true, play crucial roles in transmitting information between characters and shaping how they think about others and themselves. By quoting at length from the newspaper coverage of Holly's arrest, Capote demonstrates that even the purportedly "objective" information of the newspaper is itself prone to the same kind of errors, exaggerations, and biases as the "fictional" stories he writes, and the "fraudulent" tales Holly tells. For example, the narrator explains, Holly was arrested in his bathroom, yet the articles claim that she was found in her "glamorous apartment." The press distorts reality for its own purposes, as does Holly and, perhaps, the narrator itself. This section suggests that story telling is inherently subjective.

Summary and Analysis of Sections 14 , 15 &16

Summary

Holly is in custody, and the narrator and Joe Bell speculate as to the truth of her involvement in Sally Tomato's crime ring. The narrator tells Joe that while she did carry messages from Sally to O'Shaughnessy, she did so unknowingly, and is therefore innocent. Joe implores the narrator to contact her wealthy friends to find Holly a decent lawyer.

In the telephone booth in Joe's bar, the narrator phones O.J. Berman, who is unavailable, and then Rusty Trawler. Mag Wildwood picks up the phone, and informs the narrator that neither she nor her husband will have anything to do with that "degenerate girl." She tells him that she always knew Holly was an immoral drug addict, and that she belongs in prison. The narrator considers phoning Doc Golightly, but then remembers Holly's warning that he never reveal the secret of her marriage.

Finally, the narrator speaks to Berman, who assures him that he has already hired the best lawyer in New York, Iggy Fitelstein, for Holly's defense. Berman claims that Iggy will be getting Holly released on bail that evening, and that she may even be home already. Yet, when the narrator enters her apartment that night to feed her cat, Holly is not there, and the following morning she still isn't home. Instead, the narrator finds a strange man in the apartment packing up Jose's wardrobe. The man resembles Jose, and admits to the narrator that he is his cousin. He asks the narrator to pass a letter from Jose along to Holly, and he agrees.

Two mornings later, the narrator visits Holly in her room at the hospital where she was admitted on the night of her arrest. The vigorous horseback riding had induced a miscarriage, which, she confides, she plans on blaming on the female officer who slapped her. She also tells the narrator about "the fat woman" – an ominous figure she sees in her deepest grief. She had first appeared to Holly after she heard of her brother's death, and, with the miscarriage, she had appeared again. She asks the narrator about Jose, and he shows her the letter. She asks him to read it aloud. Before he starts, she insists on applying makeup and puts on her signature dark glasses and pearl earrings.

The narrator reads Holly Jose's letter, which explains that though he loves her, he can't afford to marry a woman involved in a public scandal as it would compromise his high professional and religious stature in Brazil. He asks her forgiveness and blesses her and her child. Holly asks the narrator's opinion of the letter, and he admits that he found it honest and touching. The narrator sees that while Holly is trying to act nonchalant, she is devastated. Holly admits that she loved "the rat."

Holly changes topic, and begins discussing her plans to sue the state for inducing her miscarriage. When the narrator pleads with her to be reasonable and "make plans", Holly confides that she is planning on skipping bail that Saturday morning. She asks him to escort her from her apartment to the airport, where she still has reservations on a flight to Brazil. When he refuses, insisting that she "stick it out," she explains that the state has no interest in prosecuting her, and that they are only interested in her testimony against Sally Tomato, which she is unwilling to give.

Moreover, she wishes to escape public scrutiny. "Certain shades of limelight wreck a girl's complexion," she says. Even if a jury found her innocent, she explains, she would have no future in New York and no prospects with the local wealthy men. Her livelihood depends on her evading the trial. Before the narrator leaves, Holly asks him to find her a list of the fifty richest men in Brazil and to search her apartment for the St. Christopher medal he gave her. She believes she will need its luck for the trip.

Analysis

At the beginning of section 14, the narrator confides that he feels Holly was turned in by Sapphia Spanella, as she had already called the authorities several times complaining about Holly. Spanella objects to Holly's behavior on moral grounds; her main concern is Holly's promiscuous behavior. In the world of the novella, filled with outcasts, eccentrics, and other unorthodox personalities, Spanella represents the moral and social status quo of mid–century America. Her vicious persecution of Holly reminds the reader that mainstream society was far from hospitable to women like Holly, whose liberal and independent lifestyles did not conform to the dominant definition of femininity.

As the narrator and Joe Bell attempt to secure help for Holly, they find that their resources are limited. In particular, her former companions, the newly married Mag and Rusty, are suddenly unwilling to help her. Mag is particularly upset at the narrator's call, insisting that she and her husband will "positively *sue* anyone who attempts to connect our names with that ro–ro–rol[vol]ting and de–de–degenerate girl." She calls her a "hop–head" (drug addict) with "no more morals than a hound–bitch in heat." While O.J. Berman hires an important lawyer for Holly's case, it is on the condition that he not be personally implicated as her benefactor. The reluctance of Holly's friends to be connected to her in her crisis reveals the dark underside of Holly's seeming popularity. While Holly had been explicit about "using" her friends for money and favors, it appears that these people had also been using her, perhaps to bolster their own status on the New York social scene.

In contrast to her fickle society friends, Joe and the narrator remain dedicated to helping Holly, suggesting that their affection for her is sincere; an interesting dynamic when we consider the ways in which these characters differ from the people Holly typically chooses for friends. Both characters are gay, thus lacking a sexual connection to Holly, and poor, thus lacking a financial connection to her. The loyalty of Joe and the narrator in this section validates the relationships between gay men and women, demonstrating the strength of love that is not founded on sexual or financial need. Aware of the insincerity of need–based affection, the narrator is not surprised when, in section 15, he finds that Jose plans to abandon Holly via a letter, unwilling to even see her again.

Section 16, set in the hospital where Holly is recovering from her miscarriage, explores Holly's pathology in depth. Unable to discuss her sadness and fear directly, she invents another metaphor, the "fat woman", to explain her depression to the narrator. She confides that it was the "fat woman" who had overtaken her after Fred's death, and asks, "[now] do you see why I went crazy and broke everything?" Holly also defends herself against sadness with physical artifice, readying herself for Jose's letter by applying meticulous makeup, jewelry, and her signature dark glasses. As she transforms herself, the narrator notices that her child–like appearance hardens and she appears "armored." The makeup symbolizes Holly's constant attempts to "armor", or protect herself against emotion by assuming different, artificial identities. The presence of three Italian women in the hospital room, none of whom can understand English and who seem to misinterpret the narrator as Holly's lover, are figures for the external world in which Holly feels perpetually misunderstood.

While the narrator's ambiguous sexual orientation is hinted at in previous sections, section 16 offers the reader a more explicit acknowledgement that he is a homosexual. Holly addresses the narrator as "Maude," which, in the gay slang of the time, refers either to a male prostitute or a homosexual. Instead of defining the narrator outright as a homosexual, Capote identifies him with slang that would have been obscure to everyone those with intimate knowledge of the gay underworld. This subtlety, apart from protecting *Breakfast at Tiffany's* from censorship, adds an element of social critique to the novella, dramatizing the indirect and delicate way even sympathizers were forced to treat homosexuality in the hostile, homophobic milieu of war–time America.

Summary and Analysis of Sections 17 &18

Summary

On Friday, it is raining so heavily the narrator is convinced Holly's flight will be cancelled. Ignoring his warning, she escapes the hospital and waits for the narrator at Joe Bell's bar, where he has agreed to meet her after recovering some possessions from her apartment, including her jewelry, guitar, and cat. Joe advises the narrator against helping Holly, but he does so anyway, lugging her struggling cat down the block in the pouring rain.

At the bar, Joe, Holly and the narrator share a bottle of brandy. While Joe claims that he is unwilling to help her in her foolishness, he arranges a limousine for her trip to the airport, and awkwardly offers her a bouquet of flowers upon her departure. The narrator agrees to ride with Holly to the airport. In the back of the limousine, Holly changes from the riding clothes in which she had been arrested and into a dress. Due to the tension between them, the narrator and Holly don't talk, but rather peer out the car windows and drink brandy in silence.

In Spanish Harlem, a "savage, a garish, a moody neighborhood", Holly suddenly asks the driver to pull up to the curb. She steps out of the car, taking the cat with her. Telling the cat that this was the "right kind of place for a tough guy like you," she drops him on the curb and gets back in the car, ordering the driver to keep going. The narrator is stunned, and calls her a bitch.

Holly repeats the story of how she and the cat never belonged to each other, they "just met by the river one day." She explains again that they were both independent and never made each other any promises. Suddenly, however, she is overcome with grief, and when the limousine stops at a traffic light, she bolts out of the car and onto the street. The narrator follows her.

The cat is not on the corner where Holly dropped him. They search the neighborhood, but find only shady neighborhood residents, including a little boy selling a different cat for a dollar. Convinced that her cat is gone, Holly realizes that they "did belong to each other. He was mine." The narrator promises Holly he would return to the neighborhood, find her cat, and take care of it himself. She tells him that she is sad for herself, and that it was tragic to "not know what's yours until you've thrown it away." She admits that all the grief she had experienced was nothing compared to how she felt after abandoning her cat.

The next day, Holly's escape makes the headlines of the newspapers. However, when the authorities find her in Rio, there is no attempt to recover her. The narrator watches the coverage of Holly diminish, revived only once when Sally Tomato dies in Sing Sing on Christmas day of that year. In the absence of any word from Holly, the owner of the brownstone sells her possessions, and her apartment is rented out to a young man named Quaintance Smith. While he entertains as many "gentleman callers" as Holly did, Sapphia Spanella is infatuated with the young man and does not object to his disruptive behavior.

In the spring, the narrator receives a postcard from Holly informing him that she has moved on from Brazil to Buenos Aires, which she deems "not Tiffany's, but almost." She admits that she has become involved with a wealthy married man and writes that she will send an address once she finds a place to live. However, the narrator does not receive the address, which disappoints him, since he wished to let her know that he had sold two of his stories, had heard of the Trawlers' divorce, and was moving out of the brownstone. Moreover, he wanted to tell Holly that he had found her cat, behind the window of a cozy–looking home in Spanish Harlem. Happy that the cat now had a home, he wonders if Holly finally does, too.

Analysis

Section 17 narrates Holly's final day in New York. In another subtle allusion to the narrator's homosexuality, the narrator admits: "[never] mind why, but once I walked from New Orleans to Nancy's Landing, Mississippi, just under five hundred miles." Critics note that Nancy's Landing is a fictional place, intended by Capote as a code phrase for a gay resort or pick–up spot. "Nancy", in gay slang, refers to a homosexual who takes the passive, or "bottom" position during sex. Thus, the narrator's evasion – "never mind why" – serves as a coy admission that his journey to Nancy's Landing had an illicit, or taboo purpose. This reference is significant, however, beyond it's identification of the narrator's sexuality. As he admits that the walk to Nancy's Landing was "a light–hearted lark compared to the journey to Joe Bell's bar", he implies that he is willing to sacrifice more for Holly than for his sexual desires. Again, the novella demonstrates the validity and power of non–sexual relationships.

Section 17 thus continues the emphasis in section 14 on the sincere affection between Holly and the narrator, and, to a lesser extent, Holly and Joe. Joe, while claiming that he'll "have no part" of Holly's escape from the authorities, nevertheless hires a limousine to aid her flight. Like the narrator, Joe is unable to address his affection for Holly directly, and instead offers her a bunch of flowers on display in his bar. His exchange is awkward, however, and the flowers end up scattering on the floor. The flowers symbolize Joe's affection; their failure to properly reach Holly perfectly encapsulates Joe's inability to admit his love.

Section 17 also contains arguably the most memorable – and important – episode in *Breakfast at Tiffany's*: Holly's abandonment of her unnamed cat and her subsequent bout of remorse. Leaving the cat on a Spanish Harlem street, Holly intends to act nonchalantly about discarding the cat but soon becomes frantic, overeager to be rid of him. She tells the cat to "beat it" and "fuck off" and urges the driver to speed away from the street where she has left him. When the narrator expresses his disgust at this callous act, Holly explains again that she and the cat "never belonged to each other" and that they were both "independents". Nevertheless, her affection for the cat indicated that Holly's attitude toward the animal was ambivalent: while they were both "independents", they shared a home and a relationship. In fact, throughout the novella, the cat is the only consistent presence in Holly's life. By rejecting the animal completely, Holly indicates that she is again unwilling to accept a close relationship and to let something "belong" to her.

In previous sections and in her monologue in section 17, Holly indicates that she views her cat as she views herself, an essentially homeless, independent wanderer without a proper name or family. Her cruelty toward the animal thus appears to dramatize Holly's self–destructive tendencies: she acts out her anger and fear on the animal she sees as a figure for herself. Moreover, Holly's abandonment of the cat repeats her own rejection at the hands of her parents, friends, and, most recently, Jose.

However, Holly's change of heart, which inspires her to tears and sends her searching for the cat in the rain suggests there is hope for her character. Realizing that she and the cat "did belong to each other...he was mine", Holly admits that no tragedy in her life had been as frightening as "not knowing what's yours until you've thrown it away." This confession presents Holly in her most genuine, honest moment in the novella, and marks the climax of her relationship with the narrator. She admits vulnerability and love for her cat and a need for a relationship in which there is mutual belonging. Strikingly, Holly confesses that both the "mean reds" and the "fat woman" are "nothing," dismissing her usual evasive metaphors for grief in favor of directly admitting her sadness.

The concluding section of *Breakfast at Tiffany's* resolves several plot threads while leaving others open–ended. The novella returns to the frame narrative, which focuses on the question of Holly's presence in Africa. Speaking in the present, the narrator quotes from newspaper articles that documented Holly's discovery in Rio, which fortunately did not lead to another indictment. The death of Sally Tomato severs Holly's ties to the criminal case against her and the gossip surrounding her slowly dies down, resolving the plotline of Holly as a refugee. The plot thread that focused on Holly's personal struggle with identity and belonging, however, is left unresolved. The narrator reveals that while Holly wrote him soon after her escape, she had yet to find a permanent address. As he never heard from her again, he assumes that she either never found this address, or forgot about him. This turn of events refutes those of the previous section, which suggested that Holly was on the brink of a positive personal transformation. While she had recognized and acknowledged her need to love and be loved, Holly's postcard informs the narrator that she has returned to her old ways, using men for their money, unable and unwilling to find a stable home. That she did not stay in touch with the narrator retroactively casts a negative light on their friendship, and suggests that perhaps her feelings for him were not as strong as they had appeared.

Despite the rather negative ending to Holly's tale, the conclusion of the novella is positive in tone. The narrator relates that a young man named Quaintance Smith moved into Holly's apartment, where he entertained as many male visitors as Holly without the judgment of Sapphia Spanella. The mention of his many "gentleman callers", along with the name "Quaintance" – a reference to George Quaintance, a painter of the 1940s and 1950s whose art was overtly homosexual in content – suggest that the new tenant is gay, practicing an unorthodox lifestyle that links him symbolically with both Holly and the narrator and extends the novella's theme of community between sexual outsiders beyond Holly's departure.

The most positive aspect of the novella's ending, however, is that we learn that the narrator has maintained warm feelings toward his old friend. He keeps his promise to her and searches Spanish Harlem for her cat, which he sees behind the window of a homey–looking room. He muses that, along with a home, the cat likely has a name; he is "certain he'd arrived somewhere he belonged." A home and a name were, for Holly, the two signifiers of belonging, and the narrator hopes that Holly has achieved the same things. This sentiment demonstrates the narrator's continued affection for Holly even in her absence. That the novella concludes by exploring his warmth for Holly suggests that the novella was less about Holly than about how loving her transformed the narrator's own life.

Suggested Essay Questions

1. In his book The Worlds of Truman Capote, critic William L. Nance suggests that Holly Golightly belongs to a generation of "Capote heroines who have learned to preserve their integrity by safeguarding their uniqueness." Do you feel that Holly's unorthodox behavior is a way of protecting her uniqueness from the conformist demands of American society, or is it a symptom of her inability to achieve stability and maturity in her personal life? Discuss Holly's unconventional personality using at least three specific examples from the novel.
2. Names and naming are a central concerns of the novel. Holly changes her name, her cat is unnamed, and the reader never learns the narrator's name. Moreover, many names in the novella have special or symbolic meaning. Focusing on at least two characters, discuss the significance of names and naming in the text. What do their names, or lack thereof, tell us about the characters, and about Capote's own thoughts about personal identity and belonging?
3. One of the most significant lines in the novel is O.J. Berman's claim that Holly is "isn't a phony because she's a real phony...[she] believes all this crap she believes." What does Berman mean? Explore Berman's claim by examining at least three examples of Holly's "phony" behavior towards others and/or herself within the text.
4. Animals, both wild and domestic, are significant motifs in the novel. For Holly, animals often represent the kind of untamed freedom she has adopted as her own lifestyle. Horses and birds also recur in the narrative. Choosing at least one of these animals, discuss its significance to Holly's personal development. For example, you could discuss Holly's relationship with her cat as it dramatizes her journey towards finding a place in which she feels at home, or trace the different forms in which horses appear as figures for Holly's need for control over her environment.
5. Holly characterizes the narrator as having his "nose pressed against a glass": he is someone who "wants awfully to be on the inside staring out". How does Capote demonstrate that the narrator is an "outsider"? What, if anything, is he "outside" of? Discuss, making sure to explore the relationship between the narrator's "outsider" status and his vocation as a writer.
6. Critic Paul Levine has argued that the major theme of Breakfast at Tiffany's is love. He writes: "'Breakfast At Tiffany's' is a love story – of a different nature. It is concerned with all forms of love: sexual, homosexual, asexual, perhaps even spiritual." Explore Levine's claim by examining the different expressions of love in the novella, paying particular attention to the relationship between the narrator and Holly Golightly.
7. Much recent criticism on Breakfast at Tiffany's has excavated the novella's many allusions to homosexuality and the underground gay communities of mid–century New York City. Moreover, the novella contains several

references to sexual identities and practices that do not clearly fit into a gay/straight binary. Exploring the novella's treatment of dynamic and unorthodox sexualities, explain why you think Capote would have made sexual "otherness" such an important subtext in Breakfast at Tiffany's. Be sure to examine how the queer setting communicates key details about Holly and the narrator's characters.

8. For Holly, the jewelry store "Tiffany's" represents home and a sense of belonging. Yet, these are the very things that Holly fears. Trace the motif of Tiffany's as both "home" and "fear of home" throughout the text, including an extended discussion of the novella's title.
9. Much of the novella is concerned with the importance of storytelling and the (im)possibility of objective information. Is there any such thing as a "true" story in this novella? How do stories shape and transform how the characters view each other and themselves? For what purposes do characters lie, exaggerate, or omit information? Discuss with reference to at least two of the following: Holly's lying, the narrator's writing, the layered frame narratives of the first section, and the newspaper coverage of Holly's arrest. Be sure to explore how the novella's skeptical attitude toward "objective" information colors our reception of the story.
10. What attracts Holly and the narrator to one another? How are the two characters different, and how are they similar? Compare and contrast Holly and the narrator with specific reference to at least three episodes that you feel illustrate the dynamic of their friendship.
11. The film "Breakfast at Tiffany's" is in some ways similar to the novella, and in other ways, quite different. Discuss the ways in which the film departs from the novella, and explain why you believe the producers would have introduced such changes. Explain which version you feel is stronger, and why.

Breakfast at Tiffany's on Film

The 1961 film "Breakfast at Tiffany's" is far more popular than the novella it was adapted from. While the film closely follows much of the original dialogue, it does depart from the novella in several crucial ways. Screenwriter George Axelrod said of the adaptation process: "Nothing really happened in the book...[what] we had to do was devise a story, get a central romantic relationship, and make the hero a red–blooded heterosexual." Most of the major changes to the novella's plot and characters were consequences of the shift to a typical Hollywood love story. In the novella, the narrator is a private, conscientious homosexual with an unrevealed name. In the movie, this character was transformed into "Paul Varjak", a kept man who is love with Holly. The film introduced the character "Tooley" as Paul's benefactor, and omitted most of the novella's references to Holly's sexual promiscuity and quasi–prostitution. While such shifts were the inevitable result of mid–century taboos surrounding sex, they also indicate how such taboos were organized around gender. The film preserves Capote's depiction of semi–prostitution, but shifts the activity from Holly to the male protagonist, in keeping with dominant double standards that accepted male promiscuity and condemned openly sexual women. Accordingly, Capote's provocative exploration of sexual difference is absent from the film version of "Breakfast at Tiffany's". The discussions of lesbianism, homosexuality, and gender that made the novella so innovative were omitted from the screenplay, and the two main characters are portrayed according to the dominant gender stereotypes of the early sixties. The film "Breakfast at Tiffany's" preserves all of Holly's signature stylistic quirks except her short, "boyish" haircut, which in the novella signified her rejection of the current feminine ideal. Most strikingly, the film revises Capote's ambiguous conclusion in favor of a romantic happy ending between Paul and Holly that conforms to the formula of mainstream Hollywood cinema.

In a letter to his aunt, Capote admitted that he had originally picked Marilyn Monroe to play the part of Holly, a suggestion the producers dismissed for "image reasons". While the choice of Audrey Hepburn, whose famous thinness matched Holly's, may have been more aesthetically appropriate, it is likely that the producers were also concerned that Monroe's overt eroticism would undermine the project of de–sexualizing Holly's character. Hepburn, widely considered the epitome of class and tact, was in fact initially reluctant to take the role because of the character's loose moral character. Nevertheless, Hepburn's turn as Holly Golightly is often considered among her best performances, and gained her an Academy Award nomination for Best Actress. Hepburn's costumes, designed by legendary designers Edith Head and Givenchy, had an immediate and profound influence on both 1960s couture style and popular women's fashion. To this day, "Breakfast at Tiffany's" is singled out as one of the greatest achievements in costume design, and Hepburn's image as Holly Golightly remains synonymous with elegant, minimalist style.

Author of ClassicNote and Sources

A. Kimball, author of ClassicNote. Completed on June 06, 2006, copyright held by GradeSaver.

Updated and revised Christina Shelby June 19, 2006. Copyright held by GradeSaver.

Plimpton, George. Truman Capote. New York: Doubleday, 1997.

Capote, Truman. Breakfast at Tiffany's: A Short Novel and Three Stories. New York: Random House, 1958.

Nance, William L.. The Worlds of Truman Capote. New York: Stein and Day, 1970.

Clarke, Gerald. Capote: A Biography. New York: Simon and Schuster, 1988.

"[Various entries]." Dictionary.com. 2006–06–06. <http://dictionary.reference.com/>.

Breakfast at Tiffany's. Dir. Blake Edwards. Perfs. Audrey Hepburn, George Peppard. DVD. Paramount Pictures, 1961.

Pugh, Tyson. "Capote's 'Breakfast at Tiffany's'". *Explicator*. 61.1(2002):51.

Levine, Paul. "Book Review of Breakfast at Tiffany's." The Georgia Review 3 (1959): 350–352

Essay: Breakfast at Tiffany's: A Window Into the 1950's

by Brook Jolley
August 06, 2003

Truman Capote's masterpiece of American literature, Breakfast at Tiffany's, is a wonderful story about misguided love. The novel is well deserving of a place within any compilation of literature and is epically deserving of a place within a collection of women's literature, as it presents a snapshot of a very human woman from the 1950's era United States. Holly is not a woman you might want to frame, or one that you might aspire to become, foremost because her flaws are exposed for all to see. However, she most definitely is defining of a cultured woman of the American 1950's, a modern debutant, carefree and aloof. Her character is defining of the societal changes which took place during the post World War II 1950's, when women gained independence they had not previously shared with men before the war, and the growing up period which was inevitable as they learned to walk on their own, free and spirited; women gained independence, but they had not yet gained the ability to support themselves: this was a fault of the society. The novel shows this change beautifully, from the perspective of a man who falls in love with one of these new wild and spirited creatures that he does not completely understand.

The narrator, or "Fred" as he is called by Holly, is captivated by this curious and unique creature who resides in his apartment building. His first meeting, where she comes in through his fire escape to avoid a man who is biting her, seems to catch him off guard. She is brash, seeming not to care to climb into his bed to snuggle, confident in her sexuality. Throughout the novel this is a continuing theme. The women of the pre–WWII era would have been very much offended by this sort of behavior, but it seems to intrigue our narrator. As the story moves on, the narrator develops much more than a passing interest in his neighbor, falling deeply in love with her, but always knowing that she will not have him. Her story to Joe Bell in the bar is the most telling, as it seems to not be directed toward Joe Bell, but rather to "Fred," although he never seems to connect that it is meant for him. Holly tells Joe "Never love a wild thing... you can't give your heart to a wild thing: the more you do, the stronger they get." (Capote 209) "Fred" never gets the message, already blinded by his love for her. She further warns him that she will fly away if he tries to get too close, a promise she eventually keeps. Holly is a fiercely independent woman, and this makes her attractive to every man she comes into contact with.

Grave mischaracterizations of Holly are sometimes made, including the accusation that she is a whore or prostitute. Granted, her behavior is not something that will ever win her a medal. She uses most everyone she comes into contact with, either for money or simply as her playthings. She does not, however, pressure these people into her company. They rather desire to be around her. Her personality is magnetic throughout most of the novel. She is not a fantastic person, but she most definitely is a wonderful image of the type of woman people desired to be around in the 1950's era. She also did not use these people out of sheer hatefulness, but out of necessity. She had to survive childhood as a runaway in one of the hardest times in the history of the United States, obviously having no true formal education which would provide a job for her to take care of herself. She was forced to marry at the age of fourteen, again out of necessity, to find a way to provide for both herself and her brother. She later leaves the situation, not because it is unbearable, but because she wants more and she wishes to explore and live her life. These are desires shared by most everyone growing up, and while considering the circumstances most people could not fault her for her actions, it was the fault of her nature. She was a fifteen year old girl, and she was not designed to be caged.

This novel is a great story of human nature, overcoming adversity, and is a very human portrait of the post–WWII era American woman. Holly is not a perfect person, but because her flaws are bared for all to see, she is a much more identifiable and loveable character. Capote's master work would be a grave omission from any collection of literature about women.

Work Cited

Capote, Truman. Breakfast at Tiffany's. 1958. New York: Vintage, 1993.

Quiz 1

1. **Why was the narrator fond of his first apartment?**
    A. He wasn't fond of his apartment
    B. He had an interesting roommate
    C. It was the first place of his own
    D. It was large and beautifully furnished

2. **Where was Holly Golightly's apartment?**
    A. Above the narrator's
    B. Below the narrator's
    C. Above Joe Bell's bar
    D. Next door to the narrator's

3. **Which is NOT one of Joe Bell's interests?**
    A. Gilbert and Sullivan
    B. Sausage making
    C. Weimaraner dogs
    D. Ice hockey

4. **What is Joe Bell doing when the narrator enters his bar?**
    A. Crying
    B. Watching a baseball game
    C. Arranging flowers
    D. Polishing a mirror

5. **How does the narrator know I.Y. Yunioshi?**
    A. He met him travelling through Japan
    B. They were both regulars at Joe Bell's bar
    C. He lived above the narrator in the brownstone
    D. He worked with him on a picture magazine

6. **What or who is Winchell?**
    A. A neighborhood gossip
    B. An African carver
    C. A popular gossip columnist of the day
    D. A popular film star of the 40s and 50s

7. **In what village does Yunioshi find the carving of Holly?**
    A. Tococo
    B. Tococul
    C. Morroco
    D. Anglia

8. **Why does the African artist refuse to sell the carving of Holly?**
    A. It is not a carving of Holly, and does not want to cheat Yunioshi
    B. He had a relationship with Holly and treasures her memory
    C. He does not understand Yunioshi's English, and does not realize that Yunioshi is negotiating a sale
    D. He recognizes that it is a priceless work of art

9. **Why does Joe Bell refuse to believe that Holly is in New York**
    A. He has concrete proof that she is still in Africa
    B. He has walked the streets for ten years and never seen her
    C. She told him that she would never return to New York
    D. She promised that if she ever returned, she would visit him

10. **Which is the only name the narrator recognizes on the mailboxes of his old brownstone?**
    A. Sapphia Spanella
    B. Quaintance Smith
    C. I.Y. Yunioshi
    D. Mag Wildwood

11. **According to her mailbox , what is "Holly" short for?**
    A. Holcomb
    B. Holiday
    C. Holly Mae
    D. Hollywood

12. **How old is Holly when the narrator first meets her?**
    A. 17
    B. 18
    C. 19
    D. 20

13. **Why does Holly ring Mr. Yunioshi's bell?**
   A. She wasn't given a key
   B. She lost her key
   C. She wishes to talk to him
   D. She enjoys bothering him

14. **What is the name of the man accompanying Holly the first night the narrator sees her?**
   A. Rusty Trawler
   B. O.J. Berman
   C. Sid Arbuck
   D. Harry Arbuck

15. **Holly is rarely without her...**
   A. red carnation
   B. martini shaker
   C. cat
   D. dark glasses

16. **What is "21"?**
   A. A gay bar
   B. Holly's address
   C. A dancehall
   D. A restaurant

17. **On his way back from "21", the narrator sees a birdcage in a shop window. Why does it impress him?**
   A. It is palatial
   B. It is beautiful
   C. It is reasonably priced
   D. It is filled with parrots

18. **What brand of cigarettes does Holly smoke?**
   A. Virginia Slims
   B. Minarets
   C. Picayunes
   D. Picadillos

19. **Why is the narrator intrigued by the country songs Holly plays on her guitar?**
   A. She is an excellent country singer
   B. They suggest her rural roots
   C. He is a country music fan
   D. She seems to have composed them herself

20. **Why does Holly visit the narrator's apartment late at night?**
   A. She is avoiding Yunioshi
   B. She is escaping a "terrifying man"
   C. She is lonely
   D. She can't find her key

21. **Why does Holly call the narrator "Fred"?**
   A. He refuses to tell her his name
   B. He reminds her of one of her lovers, Fred
   C. He reminds her of her brother, Fred
   D. It is his name

22. **Why does Holly claim she is attracted to older men?**
   A. She has trained herself to like them
   B. She has a "father complex"
   C. Young men treat women with disrespect
   D. She adores grey hair

23. **Holly asks the narrator to tell her the plotline of one of his short stories. Why does he refuse?**
   A. He is too tired
   B. He is ashamed of his work
   C. His plotlines are too long
   D. He doesn't write the kind of stories one can tell

24. **What does Holly assume the narrator's short story is about?**
   A. Two schoolteachers
   B. Two homosexuals
   C. Two sisters
   D. Two lesbians

25. **Why does Holly wish for a lesbian roommate?**

A. Lesbians never get married
B. Lesbians are wonderful homemakers
C. She is a lesbian herself
D. Lesbians tend to be rich

Quiz 1 Answer Key

1. **(C)** It was the first place of his own
2. **(B)** Below the narrator's
3. **(B)** Sausage making
4. **(C)** Arranging flowers
5. **(C)** He lived above the narrator in the brownstone
6. **(C)** A popular gossip columnist of the day
7. **(B)** Tococul
8. **(B)** He had a relationship with Holly and treasures her memory
9. **(B)** He has walked the streets for ten years and never seen her
10. **(A)** Sapphia Spanella
11. **(B)** Holiday
12. **(B)** 18
13. **(B)** She lost her key
14. **(C)** Sid Arbuck
15. **(D)** dark glasses
16. **(D)** A restaurant
17. **(A)** It is palatial
18. **(C)** Picayunes
19. **(B)** They suggest her rural roots
20. **(B)** She is escaping a "terrifying man"
21. **(C)** He reminds her of her brother, Fred
22. **(A)** She has trained herself to like them
23. **(D)** He doesn't write the kind of stories one can tell
24. **(D)** Two lesbians
25. **(B)** Lesbians are wonderful homemakers

Quiz 2

1. **On what days does Holly visit Sally Tomato at Sing Sing?**
    A. Sundays
    B. Thursdays and Fridays
    C. Every other Wednesday
    D. Thursdays

2. **How did Sally Tomato get Holly to visit?**
    A. He asked her himself in Joe's bar before he was imprisoned
    B. He had his lawyer contact her just before he was imprisoned
    C. He had his lawyer contact her after he was imprisoned
    D. He sent her a telegram from prison

3. **What does Holly give O'Shaughnessey after she returns from Sing Sing?**
    A. Narcotics
    B. Hamburgers
    C. The traffic report
    D. The weather report

4. **What does Holly say to the narrator when he asks her why she is crying?**
    A. "I hate writers"
    B. "I hate nosiness"
    C. "I hate myself"
    D. "I hate snoops"

5. **Holly's handwriting is...**
    A. elegant
    B. childlike
    C. masculine
    D. tiny

6. **O.J. Berman was...**
    A. Holly's bookie
    B. Holly's agent in Hollywood
    C. Holly's first lover
    D. The director of Holly's first film

7. **What was the film for which Holly turned down an audition?**
   A. The Story of Dr. Wassell
   B. Breakfast at Tiffany's
   C. One Touch of Venus
   D. Wuthering Heights

8. **Rusty Trawler's father had been killed by ...**
   A. Tuberculosis
   B. A communist
   C. Nazis
   D. An anarchist

9. **How many times had Rusty been married before meeting Holly?**
   A. Two
   B. Five
   C. None
   D. Three

10. **Holly's bookshelf contains volumes on two subjects:**
   A. Yachting and hunting
   B. Baseball and yachting
   C. Horses and baseball
   D. Horses and yachting

11. **The narrator compares the "mean reds" to...**
   A. weltschmerz
   B. the blues
   C. envy
   D. angst

12. **Holly will name her cat when...**
   A. She finds a place that makes her feel like Tiffany's
   B. She doesn't believe in naming animals
   C. She gets married
   D. She owns diamonds from Tiffany's

13. **Mag Trawler has a noticable...**
   A. Lazy eye
   B. Stutter
   C. Wig
   D. Limp

14. **In her conversation with Mag, Holly describes the narrator as having "his nose pressed against a glass." What does this mean?**
   A. He is a dreamer
   B. He feels trapped and is always yearning for freedom
   C. He is a peeping tom
   D. He is an outsider, longing to be included

15. **What does Mag want Jose to do?**
   A. Give up politics and marry her
   B. Become the president of Brazil
   C. Give up politics and become an American
   D. Stop laughing in bed

16. **Why does the narrator visit Holly after she chastized him for not seeing Mag home?**
   A. He wants to tell her that one of his stories is being published
   B. He wants to apologize
   C. He wants to warn her against taking Mag as a roommate
   D. He has found her keys

17. **Why is Holly happy to have Mag as a new roommate?**
   A. Mag is a lesbian
   B. Mag is a great shoulder to cry on
   C. Mag will take on the lease and do the housework
   D. Mag introduces her to wealthy men

18. **What reason does Holly give the narrator for lying about her childhood?**
   A. She didn't want to upstage his tragic tale
   B. She didn't want to relive her traumatic memories
   C. The truth is too difficult to admit
   D. She is ashamed of her past

19. **What do the narrator and Holly steal at Woolworth's?**
   A. Cat figurines
   B. Halloween masks
   C. A bird cage
   D. Joss sticks

20. **When the narrator sees Holly at the library, of whom is he reminded?**
   A. Agnes Grubman
   B. Mildred Grossman
   C. Matilda Grossberg
   D. Mathilda Greenspan

21. **At the library, the narrator discovers that Holly has been consulting books about Brazil. What does this imply?**
   A. Holly is planning an affair with Jose
   B. Holly is doing research for Mag
   C. Holly is studious
   D. Holly is Brazilian

22. **Why does the narrator call Holly's gift of a bird cage "dreadful"?**
   A. He can't bear to see anything in a cage
   B. He doesn't like it
   C. It is exorbitantly expensive
   D. He has no room for it

23. **When Mag and Rusty are in a Key West hospital, where do Holly and Jose go?**
   A. The West Indies
   B. Rio
   C. New Orleans
   D. Havana

24. **What is Mag's response to Holly's confession that she is a lesbian?**
   A. She moves out of Holly's apartment
   B. She sleeps with Holly
   C. She insists that Holly sleep on an army cot
   D. She buys an army cot to avoid sleeping in Holly's bed

25. **Why does Holly consider the narrator an unsuccessful writer?**
   A. His stories have no endings
   B. He exploits his personal life for material
   C. He rarely writes
   D. He doesn't make any money

Quiz 2 Answer Key

1. **(D)** Thursdays
2. **(C)** He had his lawyer contact her after he was imprisoned
3. **(D)** The weather report
4. **(D)** "I hate snoops"
5. **(B)** childlike
6. **(B)** Holly's agent in Hollywood
7. **(A)** The Story of Dr. Wassell
8. **(D)** An anarchist
9. **(D)** Three
10. **(C)** Horses and baseball
11. **(D)** angst
12. **(A)** She finds a place that makes her feel like Tiffany's
13. **(B)** Stutter
14. **(D)** He is an outsider, longing to be included
15. **(C)** Give up politics and become an American
16. **(A)** He wants to tell her that one of his stories is being published
17. **(C)** Mag will take on the lease and do the housework
18. **(A)** She didn't want to upstage his tragic tale
19. **(B)** Halloween masks
20. **(B)** Mildred Grossman
21. **(A)** Holly is planning an affair with Jose
22. **(C)** It is exorbitantly expensive
23. **(D)** Havana
24. **(D)** She buys an army cot to avoid sleeping in Holly's bed
25. **(D)** He doesn't make any money

Quiz 3

1. **Where does Doc Golightly approach the narrator?**
   A. In Central Park
   B. Hamburg Heaven
   C. In the brownstone vestibule
   D. Outside the brownstone

2. **According to Doc Golightly, what was Holly's original name?**
   A. Lula May Brown
   B. Lulamae Barnes
   C. Lillie Mae Burnes
   D. Lolamae Golightly

3. **What is Doc Golightly's profession?**
   A. Turkey farmer
   B. Dentist
   C. Dairy farmer
   D. Horse doctor

4. **What pet did Doc give Holly after he adopted her?**
   A. A horse
   B. A canary
   C. A cat
   D. A crow

5. **How did Doc track down Holly?**
   A. He was visiting New York, spotted Holly in a crowd, and followed her home
   B. She wrote to her brother, who passed her address along to Doc
   C. He hired a private investigator
   D. He remembered that she always wanted to go to New York, and looked up her address in the phone book

6. **Why does Holly refuse to divorce Doc?**
   A. Her brother would disown her
   B. She believes that the marriage wasn't legal
   C. She wants the option of returning home to him
   D. The marriage has already been annulled

7. **What does Holly realize when she is saying goodbye to Doc?**
   A. That she will never return to Texas
   B. That she still loves him
   C. That she is still Lulamae Barnes
   D. That she is a completely different person now

8. **"Never love a ---" Fill in the blank.**
   A. Traveler
   B. Woman from Texas
   C. Wild thing
   D. Thief

9. **Where is the narrator returning from when he sees the newspaper headline about Rusty?**
   A. His job
   B. A trip to the library
   C. An interview at a newspaper
   D. A meeting with his draft board

10. **Why do the sounds from inside Holly's apartment sound "unnatural" to the narrator?**
   A. He could hear Jose and Holly arguing
   B. He could hear no voices
   C. The apartment was empty
   D. He could hear Holly and Mag arguing

11. **Why is Jose worried about Holly's violent outburst?**
   A. He believes she may be crazy
   B. He is afraid she will harm him
   C. He is afraid of public scandal
   D. He is afraid she will harm herself

12. **Who sends Holly the telegram informing her of her brother's death?**
   A. An army doctor
   B. The state
   C. Doc
   D. The telegram is anonymous

13. **Why does Holly gain weight?**
   A. She learns how to cook
   B. War–time rationing has ended
   C. She is pregnant
   D. She is "letting herself go"

14. **Which is NOT something Holly buys when Jose moves in?**
   A. A pressure cooker
   B. A wok
   C. A hunting tapestry
   D. An easy chair

15. **What does Holly wish she had done for Jose?**
   A. Remain a virgin
   B. Never married Doc
   C. Learned how to cook
   D. Learned Portuguese

16. **Which statement best expresses Holly's thoughts about homosexuality?**
   A. Homosexuality is unnatural but no business of the state
   B. Homosexuality is a sin and should be outlawed
   C. Homosexuality is natural but should be persued privately
   D. Homosexuality is natural and same–sex marriages should be allowed

17. **Why does the narrator tell Holly to shut up on Brooklyn Bridge?**
   A. He senses she is lying
   B. He feels suddenly left out of her life
   C. He wants to enjoy the view of the harbor
   D. He can't bear hearing her speak about Jose

18. **What is the name of Holly's favorite horse in Central Park?**
   A. Mabel Minerva
   B. Miami Minerva
   C. Mavis Minerva
   D. Mabel Miami

19. **Why does Sally Tomato tell Holly that there "might be trouble"?**
   A. The authorities suspect that she is not his real niece
   B. O'Shaughnessy is sick
   C. O'Shaughnessy has been talking to the police
   D. The authorities have cracked his code

20. **What does O'Shaughnessy give Holly as a wedding present?**
   A. A train ticket to New Orleans
   B. $500
   C. A plane ticket to Miami
   D. $1000

21. **What does the narrator realize while riding beside Holly?**
   A. That he will not be happy without her
   B. That as long as she is happy, he is happy
   C. That she never loved him
   D. That he no longer loves her

22. **How does the group of children frighten the narrator's horse?**
   A. They try to mount the horse while it is in motion
   B. They throw rocks and whip the horse with switches
   C. They throw cans and whip the horse with their belts
   D. They shoot the horse with a BB gun

23. **Who stops the narrator's runaway horse?**
   A. Holly and a mounted police officer
   B. He manages to stop it himself
   C. A mounted police officer
   D. Holly

24. **What does Holly call the narrator when he confesses his love for her?**
   A. "Damn fool"
   B. "Perfect darling"
   C. "Darling fool"
   D. "Perfect fool"

25. **After Holly kisses the narrator on the cheek, what happens?**

A. He faints

B. He kisses her back

C. Holly is arrested

D. Holly faints

Quiz 3 Answer Key

1. **(B)** Hamburg Heaven
2. **(B)** Lulamae Barnes
3. **(D)** Horse doctor
4. **(D)** A crow
5. **(B)** She wrote to her brother, who passed her address along to Doc
6. **(B)** She believes that the marriage wasn't legal
7. **(C)** That she is still Lulamae Barnes
8. **(C)** Wild thing
9. **(C)** An interview at a newspaper
10. **(B)** He could hear no voices
11. **(C)** He is afraid of public scandal
12. **(C)** Doc
13. **(C)** She is pregnant
14. **(B)** A wok
15. **(A)** Remain a virgin
16. **(D)** Homosexuality is natural and same−sex marriages should be allowed
17. **(B)** He feels suddenly left out of her life
18. **(A)** Mabel Minerva
19. **(A)** The authorities suspect that she is not his real niece
20. **(B)** $500
21. **(B)** That as long as she is happy, he is happy
22. **(B)** They throw rocks and whip the horse with switches
23. **(A)** Holly and a mounted police officer
24. **(A)** "Damn fool"
25. **(A)** He faints

Quiz 4

1. **What is NOT one of the newspapers in which Holly's arrest is publicized?**
    A. The Daily News
    B. The Daily Mirror
    C. The New York Times
    D. Journal–American

2. **Which is NOT one of the words the newpapers use to describe Holly?**
    A. Starlet
    B. Call–Girl
    C. Playgirl
    D. Glamour Girl

3. **O'Shaughnessy is not a lawyer, but a...**
    A. Ex–judge
    B. Defrocked priest
    C. Pimp
    D. Corrupt cop

4. **What does Holly claim both she and Sally Tomato believe in?**
    A. His innocence
    B. Justice
    C. Sobriety
    D. God

5. **Why does one newspaper article claim Holly has a drug addiction?**
    A. She admitted to having used cocaine
    B. She admitted to taking asprin
    C. She admitted to having used marijuana
    D. She admitted to drinking brandy

6. **What, according to the narrator, was the main error in the newspaper coverage of Holly's arrest?**
    A. She had been arrested in his bathroom, not in her own apartment
    B. She had been arrested in her apartment, not in Central Park
    C. She did not have a drug addiction
    D. She was not a "movie starlet"

7. **Who brings the police officers to Holly?**
   A. Yunioshi
   B. Sapphia Spanella
   C. Jose
   D. Mag Wildwood

8. **Why does the female officer slap Holly?**
   A. Holly refuses arrest
   B. Holly laughs at her
   C. Holly calls her a "damn fool"
   D. Holly calls her a "bull–dyke"

9. **What does Holly tell the narrator to do as she is being arrested?**
   A. Find her St. Christopher's medal
   B. Feed her cat
   C. Pay her rent
   D. Tell Jose that she's been arrested

10. **Why do the narrator and Joe start calling Holly's friends?**
   A. Because they can't afford to hire a lawyer for Holly themselves
   B. To try to collect money for Holly's bail
   C. Because Holly has asked them to tell her friends where she is
   D. To find out more information about Holly's involvement with Sally Tomato

11. **What does Mag threaten to do to anyone who connects her name with Holly's?**
   A. Sue them
   B. Humiliate them
   C. Harm them
   D. Have them arrested

12. **Why does the narrator not phone Doc?**
   A. Doc doesn't have a phone
   B. Holly would be upset with him
   C. He can't afford the long–distance call
   D. He doesn't want to upset Doc

13. **What is the name of the lawyer Berman hires for Holly?**
A. I.G. Fickelstein
B. Iggy Fitelstein
C. Figgy Itelstein
D. Ziggy Icklestein

14. **Who is the man in Holly's apartment the morning following her arrest?**
A. Jose's brother
B. Jose's political advisor
C. Jose's valet
D. Jose's cousin

15. **Why is Holly in the hospital?**
A. She had a nervous breakdown
B. She tried to commit suicide
C. She had a miscarriage
D. She has pneumonia

16. **What does "the fat woman" represent to Holly?**
A. Adulthood
B. Home
C. Love
D. Death

17. **What nationality are the other women in Holly's hospital room?**
A. North African
B. Italian
C. Canadian
D. Portuguese

18. **"Certain shades of limelight wreck a girls ---" Fill in the blank.**
A. Figure
B. Spirit
C. Future
D. Complexion

19. **Which is NOT among the things the narrator brings to Joe's bar?**
   A. Holly's guitar
   B. Holly's jewelry
   C. Holly's cat
   D. Holly's pressure cooker

20. **In which New York neighborhood does Holly abandon her cat?**
   A. Chelsea
   B. Spanish Harlem
   C. Chinatown
   D. Little Italy

21. **What does the narrator promise Holly before she leaves?**
   A. That he will write to her every day
   B. That he will never cage a wild thing
   C. That he will find her cat
   D. That he will never reveal her location

22. **On what day does Sally Tomato die?**
   A. Christmas Day
   B. Thursday
   C. Holly's birthday
   D. September 30

23. **Where does the narrator find Holly's cat?**
   A. He never finds her cat
   B. In a window in Spanish Harlem
   C. On a street in Spanish Harlem
   D. In Holly's old apartment window

24. **Who is Quaintance Smith?**
   A. The narrator's new boyfriend
   B. The tenant who replaces Holly
   C. Sapphia Spanella's new boyfriend
   D. The tenant who replaces Yunioshi

25. **Why does the narrator move out of the brownstone?**
A. He is being harrassed by Sapphia Spanella
B. He wants to buy a house
C. It is not the same without Holly
D. He believes it is haunted

Quiz 4 Answer Key

1. **(C)** The New York Times
2. **(B)** Call–Girl
3. **(B)** Defrocked priest
4. **(D)** God
5. **(C)** She admitted to having used marijuana
6. **(A)** She had been arrested in his bathroom, not in her own apartment
7. **(B)** Sapphia Spanella
8. **(D)** Holly calls her a "bull–dyke"
9. **(B)** Feed her cat
10. **(A)** Because they can't afford to hire a lawyer for Holly themselves
11. **(A)** Sue them
12. **(B)** Holly would be upset with him
13. **(B)** Iggy Fitelstein
14. **(D)** Jose's cousin
15. **(C)** She had a miscarriage
16. **(D)** Death
17. **(B)** Italian
18. **(D)** Complexion
19. **(D)** Holly's pressure cooker
20. **(B)** Spanish Harlem
21. **(C)** That he will find her cat
22. **(A)** Christmas Day
23. **(B)** In a window in Spanish Harlem
24. **(B)** The tenant who replaces Holly
25. **(D)** He believes it is haunted

ClassicNotes

GradeSaver™

Getting you the grade since 1999™

Other ClassicNotes from GradeSaver™

The Pearl
The Picture of Dorian Gray
Poems of W.B. Yeats: The Rose
Portrait of the Artist as a Young Man
Pride and Prejudice
Prometheus Bound
Pudd'nhead Wilson
Pygmalion
Rabbit, Run
A Raisin in the Sun
Red Badge of Courage
The Republic
Richard II
Richard III
The Rime of the Ancient Mariner
Robinson Crusoe
Roll of Thunder, Hear My Cry
Romeo and Juliet
A Room of One's Own
A Room With a View
Rosencrantz and Guildenstern Are Dead
Salome
The Scarlet Letter
Secret Sharer
Sense and Sensibility
A Separate Peace
Shakespeare's Sonnets
Siddhartha
Silas Marner
Sir Gawain and the Green Knight
Sister Carrie
Six Characters in Search of an Author
Slaughterhouse Five
Snow Falling on Cedars
Something Wicked This Way Comes
Song of Roland
Sons and Lovers
The Sorrows of Young Werther
The Sound and the Fury
Spring Awakening
The Stranger
A Streetcar Named Desire
The Sun Also Rises
Tale of Two Cities
The Taming of the Shrew
The Tempest
Tender is the Night
Tess of the D'Urbervilles
Their Eyes Were Watching God
Things Fall Apart
The Threepenny Opera
The Time Machine
Titus Andronicus
To Build a Fire
To Kill a Mockingbird
To the Lighthouse
Treasure Island
Troilus and Cressida
Turn of the Screw
Twelfth Night
Ulysses
Uncle Tom's Cabin
Utopia
A Very Old Man With Enormous Wings
The Visit
Volpone
Waiting for Godot
Waiting for Lefty
Walden
Washington Square
Where the Red Fern Grows
White Fang
White Noise
White Teeth
Who's Afraid of Virginia Woolf
Winesburg, Ohio
The Winter's Tale
Woyzeck
Wuthering Heights
The Yellow Wallpaper
Yonnondio: From the Thirties

For our full list of over 250 Study Guides, Quizzes,
Sample College Application Essays, Literature Essays and E-texts, visit:

www.gradesaver.com

25578113R00068

Printed in Great Britain
by Amazon